New Monologues for Men

New Monologues for Men

Edited by
GEOFFREY COLMAN

Bloomsbury Methuen Drama
An imprint of Bloomsbury Publishing Plc

B L O O M S B U R Y
LONDON · OXFORD · NEW YORK · NEW DELHI · SYDNEY

Bloomsbury Methuen Drama

An imprint of Bloomsbury Publishing Plc

Imprint previously known as Methuen Drama

50 Bedford Square	1385 Broadway
London	New York
WC1B 3DP	NY 10018
UK	USA

www.bloomsbury.com

BLOOMSBURY, METHUEN DRAMA and the Diana logo are trademarks of Bloomsbury Publishing Plc

First published 2016

Editorial notes © Geoffrey Colman, 2016

Geoffrey Colman has asserted his right under the Copyright, Designs and Patents Act, 1988, to be identified as author of this work.

British Library Cataloguing-in-Publication Data

A catalogue record for this book is available from the British Library.

ISBN: PB: 978-1-4725-7347-6
ePDF: 978-1-4725-7349-0
ePub: 978-1-4725-7350-6

Library of Congress Cataloging-in-Publication Data

A catalog record for this book is available from the Library of Congress

Cover design: Jesse Holborn

Typeset by Fakenham Prepress Soltions, Fakenham, Norfolk, NR21 8NN
Printed and bound in Great Britain

Contents

Performing Rights

All rights whatsoever in these plays are strictly reserved and application for performance etc. should be made before rehearsals begin to the following contacts. No performance may be given unless a licence has been obtained.

Actor's Lament by Steven Berkoff
Rosica Colin Limited, 1 Clareville Grove Mews, London SW7 5AH

Birthday by Joe Penhall
Judy Daish Associates Limited, 2 St Charles Place, London W10 6EG

Black Jesus by Anders Lustgarten
Curtis Brown Group Limited, Haymarket House, 28–29 Haymarket, London SW1Y 4SP

Blackout by Davey Anderson
Casarotto Ramsay & Associates Ltd, Waverley House, 7–12 Noel Street, London W1F 8GQ, rights@casarotto.co.uk

Blackta by Nathaniel Martello-White
Judy Daish Associates Limited, 2 St Charles Place, London W10 6EG

Bullet Catch by Rob Drummond
Casarotto Ramsay & Associates Ltd, Waverley House, 7–12 Noel Street, London W1F 8GQ, rights@casarotto.co.uk

Can't Forget About You by David Ireland
Alan Brodie Representation Ltd, www.alanbrodie.com, abr@alanbrodie.com

Candide by Mark Ravenhill
Casarotto Ramsay & Associates Ltd, Waverley House, 7–12 Noel Street, London W1F 8GQ, rights@casarotto.co.uk

Casualties by Ross Ericson
By professionals to Grist To The Mill Productions Ltd (info@gristtheatre.co.uk) and by amateurs to Permissions Department, Methuen Drama, Bloomsbury Publishing Plc, 50 Bedford Square, London WC1B 3DP, performance.permissions@bloomsbury.com

City Love by Simon Vinnicombe
The Agency (London) Ltd, 24 Pottery Lane, London W11 4LZ, www.theagency.co.uk

The Cow Play by Ed Harris
Berlin Associates, 7 Tyers Gate, London SW1 3HX

The Effect by Lucy Prebble
Knight Hall Agency Limited, Lower Ground Floor, 7 Mallow Street, London EC1Y 8RQ

Even Stillness Breathes Softly Against A Brick Wall by Brad Birch
United Agents, 12–26 Lexington Street, London W1F 0LE

The Grand Gesture by Deborah McAndrew
United Agents, 12–26 Lexington Street, London W1F 0LE

Hidden in the Sand by James Phillips
Independent Talent Group Ltd, 40 Whitfield Street, London W1T 2RH

A History of Falling Things by James Graham
By professionals to Curtis Brown Group Limited, Haymarket House, 28–29 Haymarket, London SW1Y 4SP and by amateurs to Permissions Department, Methuen Drama, Bloomsbury Publishing Plc, 50 Bedford Square, London WC1B 3DP, performance.permissions@bloomsbury.com

If You Don't Let Us Dream, We Won't Let You Sleep by Anders Lustgarten
Curtis Brown Group Limited, Haymarket House, 28–29 Haymarket, London SW1Y 4SP

Joe Guy by Roy Williams
Alan Brodie Representation Ltd, www.alanbrodie.com, abr@alanbrodie.com

The Kindness of Strangers by Curious Directive
Curious Directive, info@curiousdirective.com

Land of Our Fathers by Chris Urch
United Agents, 12–26 Lexington Street, London W1F 0LE

A Life of Galileo by Bertolt Brecht, adapted by Mark Ravenhill
Alan Brodie Representation Ltd, www.alanbrodie.com, email: abr@alanbrodie.com

Playing With Grown-ups by Hannah Patterson
By professionals to Curtis Brown Group Limited, Haymarket House, 28–29 Haymarket, London SW1Y 4SP and by amateurs to Permissions Department, Methuen Drama, Bloomsbury Publishing Plc, 50 Bedford Square, London WC1B 3DP, performance.permissions@bloomsbury.com

Red Velvet by Lolita Chakrabarti

The Agency (London) Ltd, 24 Pottery Lane, London W11 4LZ, www.theagency.co.uk

The Resistible Rise of Arturo Ui by Bertolt Brecht, translated by George Tabori and revised by Alistair Beaton
Alan Brodie Representation Ltd, www.alanbrodie.com, abr@alanbrodie.com

Skin Tight by Gary Henderson
Playmarket, New Zealand, agency@playmarket.org.nz

Sucker Punch by Roy Williams
Alan Brodie Representation Ltd, www.alanbrodie.com, abr@alanbrodie.com

True Brits by Vinay Patel
Sayle Screen Limited, 11 Jubilee Place, London SW3 3TD

Wasted by Kate Tempest
Fox Mason Ltd, 36–38 Glasshouse St, London W1B 5DL

The Whisky Taster by James Graham
Curtis Brown Group Limited, Haymarket House, 28–29 Haymarket, London SW1Y 4SP

Introduction

The choice of speech can overly preoccupy even the most experienced actor when asked to present one for audition. Many work hard to unearth ever more obscure or astounding extracts, as if freakishness will give edge or value. However such effort reveals nothing of actual use or benefit. A speech should be selected only if it enables a simple, clear route into the actor's imaginative realm. It should enable the useful demonstration of both creative and technical abilities and allow the actor to enter its imaginary world without a fight. Equally – from my own perspective as a director, coach and acting teacher – I have found that actors should generally avoid 'putting on' voices and much worked upon accents unless specifically required, for they always tend to upstage both actor and speech. Avoidance should also be the key rule where props are concerned.

Each speech in this collection is set in its performance context and accompanied by notes intended to open up possibilities for the actor, encouraging them to ask questions and to make informed and imaginative decisions about their character and their performance. My interest here is not literary criticism but rather how a piece of theatre gets into the space. This book is not, therefore, an instruction manual, but a series of markers on a creative map that doesn't really exist until you, the actor, start to put down the coordinates.

It is a rare thing indeed to be asked to audition in silence, whatever the context. In our own lives we negotiate the very act of 'being', thinking through both silence and also crucially through language – the absence of silence. Ideally, the audition process would embrace both aspects of this personal and public negotiation, but more typically (in the early stages, at least) it focuses on the immediate 'close up' of the spoken moment. The monologue is the necessary bit of the deal – the bit that actors have to get right, often in the space of 120 seconds. As an isolated piece of text, the audition speech could be seen as nothing more than a functional cultural phenomenon – an oddity or transaction solely created for a synthetic awkward moment.

Books containing audition monologues will have necessarily been through the rather sordid editorial process of cutting speeches out of existing plays, unless they have been especially written, like the grandiose patter of the old vaudevillian[1] turn. Cutting the spoken word – from the

---

[1] The vaudevillian monologist was a prized and popular entertainer in the theatres of the late nineteenth and early twentieth centuries where Music Hall and Variety entertainment craved both the salacious and the sentimental. The tradition went into decline after the First World War and subsequent rise of cinema.

moment it was necessary to speak it – is fraught with problems both editorially and theatrically. In the wrong hands, thoughts selected and edited form their cast iron emotional narratives and clear beginning, middle and end can remain like stolen, potentially useless limbs separated from a whole dramatic body. For the actor, the skill required when preparing a monologue for audition or performance is to bring the whole body back to life with the use of just one limb. Such a task is complex and virtually impossible in that an entire play cannot be assumed into the space of the two mythical minutes of an audition speech – nor should it be. A new world will need to be created: a world that breathes the memory and same oxygen of its former completeness, but a world that will necessarily be autonomous in shape and form.

It might be useful at this point to clarify what is actually meant by the terms 'monologue', 'soliloquy' and 'speech', for they are so interchangeably used that their resulting definitions are promiscuously vague and unhelpful. Of course in general terms, a speech is in some ways formal, in that it is usually delivered to a group of people or audience. It is not usually connected to, or part of anything else. The Political speech, Queen's speech, or even Best Man's speech exists outside of the more usual utterances of the politician, monarch or nervous best man, because these are constructed. As a literary term, 'monologue' has been so variously appropriated that – outside of academic study – it has come to mean all things and nothing. Simply put, a monologue is an extended set of spoken thoughts, ideas or reflections. Sometimes also called an 'interior monologue', it is uttered from the more usual interior world of hidden thought and is therefore uniquely experienced in performance by the world that has the rare privilege to hear it. In contrast, a 'dramatic monologue'[2] is not explicitly concerned with the hidden or interior moments of being, but is where a character speaks to another character. Hidden thoughts may be revealed, but they are offered as opposed to witnessed. Of course countless other labels abound, but they are more concerned with literary criticism and function and not the performance moment. But of the multitude, the label 'narrative monologue' should also be noted here. This is where a character quite literally tells a story, usually about something that has happened in the past. The Elizabethan or Jacobean monologue is more typically and correctly described as 'soliloquy' – that is when a character speaks the very private world of their thoughts as only witnessed by the audience or camera. ('To be or not to be' etc.) Again, all are essentially the same, but the correct

---

[2] Robert Browning's 'My Last Duchess' (1842) is a very good example of the dramatic monologue.

identification of the type of speech may usefully offer the actor some essential clues into the dramatic sense of the performance moment. As in life, hidden thoughts are often very different to shared thoughts.

When confronted by the excitement and possibility of so many speeches, I imagine a sort of 'extract vertigo' may gradually overwhelm even the sturdiest of performers. So many choices will not necessarily give the much hoped for instant or direct hit – a eureka moment where all aspects of craft and ambition are usefully located in just nineteen lines. Speeches may blur and congeal into a mass of words short circuiting the hunt and rendering a form of performance blindness which can be very dispiriting. But to put this into context, if this book were a compilation album of last year's greatest hits, it would be very unusual for the listener to celebrate and adore each and every piece of music with the same passion or interest. A silent filter in our heads sifts music into various emotional stacks, graded by the nearness or distance to one's own taste. Similarly, therefore, it would be unimaginably strange if each speech published here is the best one you have ever read or the one that you simply must perform. There will of course be some that will not even be read to completion and others that will be dwelt upon and cherished for years to come. Selection is primarily driven by personal preference, but it may have to be governed by particular professional requirements as stated by those holding the audition or workshop – requirements such as period, genre, performance style, language, accent, status, role, etc. The list could go on.

To select and perform a solo speech is not only to offer an immediate characterful outpouring, but to also convey technical ability, craft and skill. The monologue is not a time to demonstrate what might be: it should demonstrate what is. There may well be an ageing King Lear or Lady Macbeth in the furthest point of your career, but the director, acting coach or audition panellist will require you to be very much in the present. A speech is not in that sense a future forecast but an accurate measure of the possibility of 'now'. Selection should be about finding words and ideas that create the enabling conditions for you to show the best of your creative response to character.

In a recent conversation with playwright Simon Stevens, I asked him if, when writing, he saw the actual physical worlds of his plays: the sky, the rooms and buildings of the incredible, beautiful, dangerous places that he imagines. His answer was striking in that, for a writer of such vivid sensual and emotional skill, he said that what he actually saw was 'just the theatre,' just the machine itself: a black floor, walls, lights and rows where the audience sit. His theatre is thus a provocation for both actor and audience member to place imagination at the centre of the creative moment. As you read through these speeches you may have to make a similar decision: The machine or the physical world? You will need to be vigilant and carefully analyse any implied dramatic conventions as demonstrated through the use of stage space. The fictional 'real world' space with its sky, grass, towering building or battlefields is also very dependent on the actor's understanding of the social and cultural meaning of the world that will be inhabited. The necessity for the actor to identify spatial and aesthetic context is discussed in much of Stanislavki's famous writings, where the character's world is utterly dependent on the Given Circumstances. The challenge is quite an extraordinary one: to bring to life the physical and emotional world of a play – the union of creative and technical skill – performed in seconds.

The successful realisation of a 'truthful' audition seems to be increasingly only attainable through the successful performance of what could be described as a generalist or tele-visual performance style. Or, to put it another way, 'camera-real' acting: the acting that we see on our TV screens every day. Somehow, because it is the style we are most exposed to, it equates to a notion of good acting, and therefore by default, non-camera-real or abstract acting styles not seen on television equate to that of bad acting. When selecting possible speeches from this volume I would really urge you to consider that not all of them can be – or even should be – performed in the same way. How can they be performed irrespective of style or period? These speeches will require a sort of performance alertness if they are to be 'real'.

Geoffrey Colman

Actor's Lament by Steven Berkoff

Oh David, what a simple awful plight,
To see your work abused, made trite,
By some mad actor's ego running rampant.

Actor's Lament was given a pre-Edinburgh Festival 'try out' at the Sinden Theatre, Tenterden, on 13 February 2013, and then subsequently opened at Assembly Hall, Edinburgh, on 5 August 2013. It was directed by Steven Berkoff.

Context

This very brief one-act play (one of nineteen new Berkoff plays published by Methuen Drama in 2013) is an audacious glorious return in style to the more familiar verse plays written earlier in his career. This lamentation is as melancholic as it is acidic, those who auditioned who never got the part, the lousy directors, the talentless actors and awful plays of a career in the theatre. All is here. As affectionate as it is repulsive, Berkoff leaves no margin for doubt – working in the theatre is tough!

Acting notes

The character David seems to sum up the sheer terror and delight of the pre-performance moment; the seconds before walking into a scene. Beautifully observed, and written in verse, this speech offers the actor an opportunity to demonstrate both technical as well as emotional technique. The gathering anxiety of the approaching performance moment is accompanied by ever more crisp language structures that almost beat out the actor's thundering heart. Berkoff's work allows for a performance style which is non-naturalistic, larger than the more typical low-key televisual acting we see nightly on our screens. Such monologues can lead to flabby second-hand demonstration of a style so exactly owned by the great master himself. Every gesture, every rolled 'r' in Berkoff's performance has weight because of its authentic lineage, spanning many decades. To perform like him is not really to perform anything much at all. The task here is to bring living thought to the character David, not to create a sort of morbid tribute show for the writer. Why is David still so passionate about performance in spite of its many challenges; is he deluded or an idealist? Surely experience would temper his beating heart and his last swallow before speaking? It seems not. What does this tell us about his nature? David states that he could not live if he left the stage. Is this affectation or the true imprint of an artist?

Urbane, sophisticated, successful, forty to fifty

John   No! No! No! No! Stop! It's not so grim …
Dear God, you make it sound a living death.
An actor ages, who can turn back time?
The autumn curls our leaves and winter chops us down,
And no one can escape death's filthy leer …
The grim reaper beckons for your crown,
But not before you've left your searing mark,
Upon the citizens of this once so glorious town.
You leave your reputation, your enduring myth,
Forged from so many thousand gut-wrenched nights.
The curtain rises like a serpent's hiss,
Your heart is pounding and your tongue is dry,
The Tannoy calls … 'Beginners, places please … '
Your feet are turned into lead, your stomach mud,
Your hands are shaking and your sweat is cold,
The audience, that great and unknown mob,
Is calmly waiting for it to unfold,
Unaware that standing in the wings,
Is an actor, a trembling mass of fear,
You're waiting, waiting, several minutes more,
For late arrivals threading through the door,
The other actors smile as if they felt so fine,
Meanwhile their bladder's working overtime,
You run the first lines in your head to reassure
Yourself that they are safely bedded there.
Be careful, don't anticipate, take care!
Lest when you get right to that scene,
You'll find the lines have vanished in the air!
They're stored in your unconscious ready to explode,
But not if you keep testing them, they won't …
So hold back, just relax, although you want to bolt!
This is the time, the dreaded time, the living hell,
When actors wish they could just bloody walk,
Escape into the street where other feet
Are calmly strolling, or drinking café latte,
If only you could join them, oh what bliss,
But if you fled the stage, what bloody shame!
How could you even live another day?

Birthday by Joe Penhall

You have no concept whatsoever of the
pain, of my pain – male pain – man pain.

Birthday was first performed at the Royal Court Jerwood Theatre
Downstairs, London, on 22 June 2012. It was directed by Roger Mitchell.

Context

Joe Penhall's tenth play, a black comedy, is all breaking waters, labour
and hospital beds, but middle-class parenting could not be more unusual
though, for it is the man and not the woman who is giving birth. Penhall
presents a very modern couple who have decided to 'take it in turns' to
allow Lisa to focus on her career, and so it is up to husband Ed to deliver
the goods this time. Penhall has previously written about parenthood,
notably with *Haunted Child*, which explores the utter devastation of
parental abandonment. There is nothing immaculate about Ed's final
trimester: 'How could you forget my f***ing raspberry leaf tea?' he
screams. Penhall presents a delightfully Kafkaesque vision, not only
of male conception but also the NHS systems that will support and
ultimately (in this case) host the delivery, without an anaesthetist! Lisa,
his wife, is not much support either, and why should she be, she bore their
first child. It's payback time. Women don't seem to care much at all really,
be it Lisa or the wonderfully bored midwife. Ed will have to go it alone,
dig in deep and just get on with it. He had better not make a fuss.

Acting notes

This short speech is all about delivery. In both senses! Technically it
requires the actor to grab hold of the overarching hard-done-by argument
and play it in a very direct way. For a comic thought to 'land' it has to
be simple, and certainly not played for laughs – that would be indulgent
and it never ever works. This speech requires the sort of preparation a
musician might bring to a musical score. It will need to be marked up and
mapped out. Comic timing is not God-given; it is the result of rigorous
preparation. Ed does rather moan, but we sense in this that at any minute
his rather petty laddish observations will give way to something far more
hysterical. We the audience must sense this growing fear and despair.

His extended description of how repulsed he was by the vision of his own wife in labour must surely expose his inner thoughts and disturbing images of his own soon-to-be birthing moment. What will his wife think of him then?

Thirties

Ed   It's worse for the man.

Lisa   (Oh poor you!)

Ed   You didn't have to stand there listening to the ear- splitting screams while one congenital fuckwit after another came in, rummaged around inside you and then fucked off for a smoke. No epidural. No doctors. You didn't see them at the end, stitching you back together, legs akimbo, marinating in your own blood and shit, great strings of blood like drool. I don't know why they invited me to watch – why do they do that? They kept showing me your vagina as if it were a *holy relic*. (*Staring into space.*) Men are visually stimulated. It's our worst nightmare. Suddenly this blissful, heavenly organ, this ravishing *jewel* you've been obsessively petting and tending and eyeing with rapture all those years becomes the most alarming, harrowing thing you've ever seen in your life! It's a wonder I'm not completely *gay* by now. Because I'm telling you, as a man, once you've had a child, once you've watched a *live human* emerge from your wife's vagina, by God you need a change of scenery.

Black Jesus by Anders Lustgarten

And do you know why I was called by that
name? Because I decided who would be
saved and who would be condemned. I took
that responsibility for others and now I take it
for myself. I am Black Jesus. I do not crawl.

Black Jesus received its world premiere at the Finborough Theatre, London, on 1 October 2013. It was directed by David Mercatali.

Context

Zimbabwe in the very near future. Black Jesus, a militia leader called Gabriel Chibamu, is being interviewed by the Truth and Justice Commission about the atrocities of the Mugabe regime. Eunice (from the Commission) asks difficult questions in the knowledge that Chibamu will face trial and must answer to the past. In his published introduction, Lustgarten states that his 'intent was to use the play … to bring up a lot of heavy horrible things that happened in Zimbabwe, things that Zimbabweans themselves lacked the opportunity to talk about', but his original ideas were just too difficult to stage. He sees this reworking of those original ideas, the play *Black Jesus,* as still quite unflinching, but a usefully more philosophical attempt at presenting the complexities of a bleakly unresolved period of Zimbabwean history.

Acting notes

Eunice Ncube is trying to interview the young Gabriel. She asks him (in the line preceding this speech) to tell her about his first mission. He accuses her of raking over his ashes to find things to later burn him with and so ignores the question. He answers by avoidance and instead describes a domestic scene from his past that acted as a trigger for his more recent violent behaviour. Part justification for his association with the Green Bombers, the speech is also a tale of a horrific attack that tested his political and personal allegiance, and subsequently informed his current fearful philosophy. There is something plausible, almost inevitable, about Gabriel's reasoning and the story certainly contextualizes his determination and absolute need of 'no going back'. Lustgarten skilfully presents us with the beating heart of a monster and, whilst not condoning his undoubted bloody past, gives us the space to reflect upon its causes. The phrase 'pure evil', often used to describe such militia men, is made redundant here. There is nothing simple Gabriel's reasoning is as complex as his actions are disturbing.

Zimbabwean, mid-twenties

Gabriel   They load you into a truck without your normal cohort, with older, more experienced men, and they blindfold you. You bump and twist along the rutted roads, your mind running through all the possibilities of where you will go, what you will be asked to do, but when they shove you from the truck and take off the blindfold, at first you do not recognise the place they have taken you. It comes to you in pieces. That is where my grandmother would prepare the *sadza* and relish, and the smell would make my stomach jump. That is where for the very first time I and a girl … (*Beat.*) Your first mission is to your home, to your family. I had an uncle who was an MDC sell-out and I had to beat him right there in the yard, in front of all his relatives, under the baobab tree where I cut my knee when I was five years old. He screamed from humiliation more than the pain. After that there was no going back. You have only one family, and it is the family of the Green Bombers.

Blackout by Davey Anderson

A small room, bright lights, white walls
a metal door. Oh my God! Imagine you
wake up in a jail cell and you don't know
how you got there.

Blackout was originally commissioned by the National Theatre and performed at the Lyttleton Theatre, London, as part of National Theatre Connections by Citz Young Co. on 4 June 2008, having been developed with the support of the Citizens Theatre, Glasgow. The theatre company, ThickSkin, later produced an award-winning tour of the play, directed and choreographed by Neil Bettles.

Context

This very short, sometimes shocking play focuses on the desperate life of a young Glasgow boy, locked up in a secure-unit cell. The problem is made worse by the fact that he can't remember how or why he got there. In a sequence of brutally-drawn monologues, which tell of violence on the estate, addiction and betrayal, the playwright Davey Anderson describes how *Blackout* is based on a true story about a young man serving a probation sentence for attempted murder. A 'funny, articulate, thoughtful, passionate' boy, according to Anderson, with a burning desire to communicate.

Acting notes

The two speeches that follow seem to have the fractured speaking and thinking logic of a verbatim play. It is as though a young man's testimony has actually been recorded and written up. Incomplete thoughts hang mid-sentence, random ideas crash into ordinary moments, and an air of the confessional abounds. This is closely observed, painful and disturbing. We are at once repulsed and compelled to listen even more. The main task here for the actor is clear – the many shards of thought have to cohere within an internal logic however seemingly abstract.

Fifteen-year-old Glaswegian

James   And you'd remember the night that it finally happened ... It was raining.

James?

That's your mum. Shouting up the stairs. You turn off the music.

I'm just away up the hospital to see your granddad. You don't respond.

D'you want to come with me? No the night, Ma.

Are ye sure?

Nah, I want to stay in and watch this film.

Well, d'you want to go up and see him the morra night? Aye, Ma. Fine. Right.

I'll tell him you were asking after him. See you later.

She goes out into the rain. You put on a slasher film. slash

chop

rip stab

Blood and guts.

You look at it blankly.

It's not enough for you any more. Then there's a knock at the door You press pause.

Open the door. Awright, James. Awright.

Whit ye daeing?

Nothing. Just sitting in my room. Is yer maw in?

Naw.

Are you on your own? Aye.

Yas, man, big Jim's got an empty! Yas!

They all crowd in. C'mon.

D'ye want a joint?

emmm

Whit ye watching? Nothing.

What's that? That's a swastika.

Whit ye daeing wae a swastika up on the wall? Are you a Nazi or something?

snigger

Aye.

They all look at you.

Whit ye intae all that for?

Cos. I'm an Aryan. I need tae protect my white blood. Oh aye. And how are ye gonnae dae that?

Wait till you see this.

You slip your hand under the bed

And you pull out a sword.

Fifteen-year-old Glaswegian

James   And then you went into school.
And you'd dae the Nazi salute in the corridors. And people would walk past you.
And they'd just look at you like
Ooff
He's a pure psycho. But it felt good.
Cos you were getting tae them. And the teachers were like Stand outside this room.
What have you got this on for? Cos I like it.
Go home and change into your uniform.
You're not allowed back into the school until you change your clothes.
So you went
Fine. It's my life. I'll wear what I want. I'll say what I want. I'll dae what I want.
And you sparked up a fag
And started walking about the school
Smoking
Acting like a hard man. Haw, look
Check the state of him.
And when the bullies saw you, instead of running away, you went
Right, who's first?
Whit you gonnae dae, ya daftie? Two seconds.
Whit?
And you went fsssssssssssss
And put the fag out on your bare skin. Who's first then?
Are you awright?
C'mon, who's gieing me the first punch? James … !
Go. I'll put my hands behind my back.
You need tae get your heid sorted oot, mate. You're no right. Then you pick up a chair
And throw it at the fucker. So he starts punching you Fists flying
They all start battering you. James!
What are you doing? That's not like you.
But you're standing there
With your face red raw.
Aw, it feels great but, din't it?

Blackta by Nathaniel Martello-White

*Get, I'm getting outta here, man, I'm getting
outta here, the lines getting blurred – it's
blurred – that line between normality and
madness is muffled.*

Blackta received its world premiere at the Young Vic Theatre, London, on
26 October 2012 and was directed by David Lan.

Context

A 'blackta' is a token black actor cast as a non-white character in a TV
drama. To be cast is to beat off stiff competition and be free of crowded
audition rooms; but as the play shamefully reveals, auditions are not
always a demonstration of talent, but of skin colour. The character Brown
in Martello-White's debut play leads ever more incredible moments of
male banter, political debate and incendiary intention among a group
of blacktas who return to the audition room time and time again for
that one elusive role: the black role. Martello-White (an actor himself),
writes a funny, sometimes disturbing satire on being a contemporary
black actor where 'the competition never stops' and where the characters
are 'always either on the attack, on the defence or playing some kind of
tactical manoeuvre'. The original setting, 'everywhere and nowhere',
suggests an immediate type of performance style; Martello-White gives
stage directions that a bell should ring between scenes as in a boxing ring
between bouts. All this makes the performance landscape quite clear,
sparse, immediate, rapid and very street contemporary. The stage space is
a place of possible encounters and stories, not limited by the timber of a
poorly-made stage set. The speech is very much that of a young assured
street orator. He is an easy speaker, whose qualities would fit the agendas
of both the political and the pulpit. The monologue reveals the character's
hard-earned wisdom which betrays harsh perspectives that could both
amuse or incite, depending on how it is performed.

Acting notes

The very naming of this character Brown might suggest a sort of
archetype which could be seen as reductive and most certainly difficult

to play. How does an archetype talk, think, breathe, move? In the case of *Blackta*, Martello-Black skilfully asserts that black actors have been wrongly overlooked for far too long and have had to compete for parts as though in some grim gameshow. The speech could, therefore, be played as if to camera, stage set or to a group of people at a rally. The play's original staging was located in the suggested familiar place of a café, with Brown speaking to his friends. It makes for an interesting enough acting challenge to rescue this character from being just a loud mouth or speech maker; however, I think that the real challenge worth thinking about is how to demonstrate both aspects – the loud mouth that we all despise and the emotionally battered young man screaming for recognition. The play concludes with Brown's belief, 'I'm gonna change everything.' What drives these words? Is it hate, fear or passion and conviction? Here we have two speeches that could so easily be shouted; ideas that could so easily be pointed without dimension but their true performance will allow the spectator or audition panel a glimpse of Brown's all but destroyed fragility.

Contemporary/young black

Lights up. A cafe. DING! DING!

Black, **Dull Brown** *and* **Yellow** *are seated, whilst* **Brown** *stands. He is in mid flow.*

Brown Don't you realise – guyz! If we were born a century ago, fuck it – a few decades ago – we'd literally be slaves – slaves to an idea, thought up by the evilest of floppy heads, that we are black, and therefore worth nothing! I mean damn, now, right now, I see an army of sleeping giants, we are the enemy within. Now don't get me wrong, essentially, when it comes down to it, at the very core of this ting, is the white elite, who've had a hold of the reins of power since, day dot, well, not day dot – civilisations rise and fall – but anyway I digress, forget the white working class, their racism is amateur, based on stupidity, fear, and built on bricks of ignorance – laughable, not worth the thinking on't – we surpassed them years ago … look, what I'm saying is, we escaped hell, and are dwelling in limbo, but there's a route, a route, if we're brave enough to walk it! A route that leads to heaven! A route to power, coz let's face it, every black knows, by nature, in his nature, is a sensual magical power. But it needs to be channelled, it needs a focus, a direction, or this very power, this untamed magic, this wayward sorcery, will backfire, implode and ultimately destroy us.

Beat.

You get me?

Contemporary/young black

Brown   You see ... that's been your problem ... from the start
... everywhere you go, you make enemies, an' I think, well you're
intelligent, articulate, why the fuck can't this guy take a break? You
know? Why doesn't he get, that if history has taught us anything, it's
that great men always had a team of people who respected them, men
who were so inspired by this great man, that when they woke from
slumber, they would think – how would black brush his teeth? What
does black eat for breakfast? Man how is black?

Does he need anything? Man, I wish I waz like black, I wish I waz
black, I hope he's OK ... .Then all of a sudden, you got all this
positivity, being pumped into the universe, like a protective force field,
even God thinks – I want this guy to do well! Let me give him what he
needs to achieve his dream, a good woman, good luck, good health, I
mean black man – come on ... that's how you make it! That's how you
get the greenest of ever green lights – every time! Do you take sugar in
your tea?

Black   (Yeah, two thanks – yer right –)

Brown   Right, you see, you and yellow, have the same problem, you're
like these two big grunting ogres, who trudge about the place, expecting
respect, now that's not how you get respect ... you know that! I mean
you earn respect man ... take the three of us, you, me and yellow ...
between the three of us, the things we've done – we're powerful man,
damn look at all the things we've done

Bullet Catch by Rob Drummond

*The Bullet Catch is really pretty simple. A bullet is marked
and loaded into a firearm. The firearm is given to an
assistant, whether predetermined or newly acquired from
the audience.*

Bullet Catch was first performed at The Arches, Glasgow, in 2009 as part
of the BEHAVIOUR festival. Written, co-directed and performed by Rob
Drummond (the other director being David Overend), the play transferred
to The Shed at the National Theatre, London, on 21 May 2013.

Context

Bullet Catch is an imaginative piece of old-fashioned vaudevillian entertainment, a magic show that would befit any theatre of the Victorian
period. And yet it also captures the current fascination for David Blaine-
or Derren Brown-type mentalism – in this case, how to catch a bullet fired
from a loaded gun. Drummond re-imagines this famous (and deadly) trick
through the story of illusionist William Wonder and explores its tragic
cultural history and the life of its protagonist. The finale is both inevitable
and breathtaking – a volunteer from the audience is persuaded to actually
shoot a 'loaded' gun into the face of the performer. The play gained
near mythic status when first performed in 2009 and continued to gather
awe-struck adulation when at the National Theatre in 2013.

Acting notes

The acting challenges are quite complex. The showman and performer
manipulates both the emotional tension of the 'trick' and, through this
premise, expertly controls the hearts and minds of the audience, overriding
any sense of their rational or logical ability to process, demanding that
they suspend their natural cynicism for such acts. The speech is at once
a history lesson, a sales pitch, clever shtick and foolish banter. There are
the facts but are they really facts? There is the Houdini letter but did he
really write it? The performance is haunted by many voices and ghostly
instructions. The actor needs to master this complex relationship with
many elements of narration without seeming smug or showy. The magic
set-up has to be humanized as well as being allowed to be unreal.

Lisa   Does everyone know what a Bullet Catch is?

The Bullet Catch is really pretty simple. A bullet is marked and loaded into a firearm. The firearm is given to an assistant, whether predetermined or newly acquired from the audience.

Wonder *gives the mobile phone to* **Lisa**.

The assistant, carefully, takes the weapon and holds it in the safety position.

Wonder *shows* **Lisa** *the safety position, the 'gun' pointed away from her feet towards the ground and never at the audience.*

The assistant then stands on a designated spot.

Wonder *places* **Lisa** *on her spot.*

The magician takes up his position …

Wonder *stands opposite her.*

… and encourages the assistant to aim at his mouth.

Wonder *encourages* **Lisa** *to aim the phone.*

And when the magician gives the signal – sometimes verbally, but in Henderson's case by lowering his arm from above his head to his side – the assistant squeezes the trigger, sending a bullet hurtling at five hundred miles per hour towards the magician's head with a loud bang.

Wonder *drops his hand to his side and waits to see if* **Lisa** *will take the initiative and make a 'bang' noise. She does. It is comically weak. He thanks her and invites her to take a seat onstage.*

Usually this is followed by the magician staggering backwards before revealing the marked bullet between his teeth. But it doesn't always happen this way. In 1613 the inventor of the stunt, Coullew of Lorraine, was accidentally shot in the head when his assistant – who also happened to be his wife – decided to down half a bottle of absinthe before the show to calm her nerves. Arnold Buck in 1840 died when a volunteer secretly loaded nails from his pocket into the barrel of the gun. And Raoul Curran, forty years later, successfully accomplished the stunt only for an audience member to stand up, take out his own pistol and shout 'Oi, Curran, catch this'.

There's a reason this is known as magic's riskiest stunt. When William Henderson declared he was going to attempt it in London using an audience member to pull the trigger, his friend and mentor Houdini wrote to him.

Wonder *takes out a letter.*

Now, my dear boy, this is advice from the heart, don't try the damned Bullet Catching, no matter how sure you may feel of its success. There is always the biggest kind of risk that something will go wrong. And we can't afford to lose Henderson. You have enough good material to maintain your position at the head of the profession. And you owe it to your friends and your family to cut out all the things that entail risk of your life. Please, William, listen to your old friend Harry who loves you as his own son and don't do it. You have too much to lose. You are free to choose not to do this.

This last line is delivered directly to **Lisa**.

Of course, Henderson ignored this advice and one hundred years ago was killed instantly in front of two thousand people at the London Palace Theatre when kind, mild- mannered labourer Charles Garth shot him in the face.

Can't Forget About You by David Ireland

I mean I know I have only just met but you
seem so normal – and you and your family,
and all the other people I meet here, I think
how did any of you manage to grow up
normal?

Can't Forget About You received its world premiere at the Lyric Theatre, Belfast, on 19 May 2013 and was directed by Conleth Hill.

Context

Though labelled a 'romantic comedy', *Can't Forget About You* doesn't ever retreat from more urgent themes which include sectarianism, the future of Northern Ireland and cultural identity. We encounter Belfast-born Stevie, a twenty-five year old politics graduate and an older Glaswegian widow, Martha, who rather extraordinarily invites herself into his life and then into his bed ('Would you like to have sex with me?'). This seems to be the perfect solution for it does without the complexities of a long courtship. Martha is not looking for anything long lasting and neither is Stevie. Or so it seems. But love, not lust, flourishes in the wake of their sexually-convenient relationship. The play's knowing humour is both touching and edgy in equal measure, notably the awkward generational exchanges between the much older Martha, younger Stevie and his family. This is difficult territory in that it inhabits the toe-curling truths of an inevitable and exasperated type of cynicism residing within a dysfunctional, difficult relationship where awkward sex not only provokes a set of domestic questions ('And fuck the age difference'), but by so doing also agitates painful stories from Ireland's past and present.

Acting notes

Stevie is sleeping with a woman many years his senior, who struggles with her past, her morality and the death of her husband. She is in therapy and confesses to feeling 'like some haggard old witch' as she struggles, in between acts of ever increasing degradation, to live in the present. This is all rather new and overwhelming territory for young Stevie, who is just a little unsettled by his lover's constant references to her dead husband (especially when they have sex). He needs to work out what Martha is searching for but *he* also needs to work out what he is actually searching for. Is he using Martha or loving her? And what will his mum say? The task for the actor playing this extraordinary role is to identify a simple route through Stevie's reasoning. Most young men of his age would not date someone as old as their mother, let alone sleep with them. Is sex on tap a sort of displacement activity, putting his life on hold, or is it his part of an essential journey towards discovery? Once discovered, will he move on from Martha?

Irish, a young man

Stevie   I'm really happy with you.

Every time I see your face I feel like a better person. I feel like the person I was always meant to be.

I think you're my soulmate.

And I never believed in anything like that before I met you. And I think you're scared. Yes, scared of the age difference but also about Jim.

I think your husband's death, I think it scared you, it scared you more than you think. I think you're scared of falling in love again, you're afraid of being hurt, you're afraid of going through that kind of pain again.

And so am I. OK? So am I.

I know you think I'm too young and I don't know anything about love or life or relationships. But I know what happened to my mother after my father died, how devastated she was by his death. And I watched my sister get divorced from the love of her life, her childhood sweetheart. I watched all that so give me some credit, OK, I know something.

And I don't care if this relationship lasts one year or five years or ten years or a hundred years. I want it. I want you in my life, no matter what.

And I am a Buddhist. OK? Despite what youse all say about me, I am a Buddhist

And Buddha tells us we should live in the now and I want us to live in the now, Martha, and embrace this moment and embrace each other and embrace the joy of being alive.

And my toe is really sore right now and I think I'm going to faint.

Candide by Mark Ravenhill

Some time ago
I conducted a certain scientific experiment
With a chambermaid.

Candide received its world premiere at the Swan Theatre, Royal Shakespeare Company, Stratford-upon-Avon on 29 August 2013 and was directed by Lyndsey Turner.

Context

Voltaire wrote the novel *Candide* in 1759 in an effort to 'satirise the views' of the philosopher Leibniz, who had stated that life was organized by a grand designer, and who methodically optioned different worlds before putting the human species in the 'the best of all possible worlds'. This is the story of a young aristocrat and his tutor journeying across the world hoping to prove that, in spite of human cruelty and natural disaster, 'everything is for the best'. Ravenhill uses a dramatic structure that shifts between the eighteenth and twenty-first centuries with scenes set in the past, present and near future.

Acting notes

The first of two the speeches selected from this play is a beautifully-pitched reminiscence that dances around both the past, with its clearly identifiable state control, and the current time, in which the character Mike isn't even sure which continent he is on when he wakes up. The glorious past that has created so much work for generations to come but, in doing so, has neutered the present by its opportunism and ultimate burden. As ever with Ravenhill's work, it seems deceptively easy on the page. The challenge here is to reveal a layered emotional state that both cherishes and despises what has gone before, but also accepts the present while being critical and ultimately bewildered by it. First we have a speech written that feels quite spontaneous, but is (in fact), not a speech at all. This is difficult.

The second speech is that of Voltaire, who actually speaks only once in the entire play. It was he (Francois-Marie Arouet, known as Voltaire), who was moved to write his philosophical tale *Candide* by the loss of approximately 100,000 lives in an earthquake in Lisbon. The balance of statesman-like rhetoric fused with quite extraordinary visual and evocative language ('Mountains of corpses, women, children – dead') is the challenge. Another is how to humanize the experience of such a catastrophe while celebrating the period language, a pseudo-antique rhyming verse form. How can this go beyond being a wordy historical account?

Mike   When I was growing up, wasn't just the photos
   that were black and white
Every bit of life
Fixed
Living in a country that was – basically –
socialist. Glasses on your nose – chosen by the
state. Everything driven by a hatred
Of individuality.
Stretching before me –
(We grew up without a hope or aspiration) –
Was a life-long job with some council or
corporation. I was carrying bins
– dirty, heavy – from the doorstep to the
cart. For ever. One day
'They're gonna privatise the bins'.
I could see this was the only chance I'd ever
have. Put in a bid – got the investors –
And now
This job that once we did as serfs
Was ours.
Working day and night.
Hiring, firing. Fighting,
Driving out the unions. Finally an offer
That we couldn't refuse:
Sell to a conglomerate, Swedish
based. I'm a name your price
consultant.
I wake up every day before it's light
Never quite
Sure which country, continent I'm in,
So much work to do –
Not only for your generation but for generations
   after you –

Voltaire   Approach my friends and stop and see
Walls toppled, buildings of lost dignity
Which now crush men beneath their stone and lead Mountains of
corpses, women, children – dead. Voices calling 'Help me' with their
final breath Torment unimaginable, forcing death.
When we hear these weak and frightened cries
Break from the ashes, see the smoke arise
Can we proclaim eternal verity, Believe a God allows this cruelty?
Can we look upon this bloody, broken sight
And say that any God would find it right?
Was it because she strayed or sinned or swore
That this mother clasps and wails her infant's corpse? We say: This
fallen city can be soon rebuilt
New humans through its streets will surely spill And always wealth is
made. It's understood Some suffer now but all is for the greater good.
Our words are nothing, a bitter sound,
Salt rubbed and rubbed again into a wound. We must not argue a great
eternal cause
Say this was pre-ordained by Heaven's laws. I see chaos, chance, a
universe of cruelty, Evil – all things denied in our philosophy.
I cannot say our current state is right: But I will learn to bear this
present life. Believing after universal pain, tears, strife This darkness
shall be turned to light.

Casualties by Ross Ericson

So what?
So what if he was a dog?
It could have been any of us.
I was on the other side of that wall when that
thing went up. I stood there and watched as
lumps of burnt flesh landed all around me.

Casualties received its world premiere at the Park Theatre, London, on 18 June 2013 and was directed by Harry Burton.

Context

Afghanistan. A counter-IED team deal with keeping the peace and holding their nerve. In the introduction to the play, playwright Ross Ericson (who briefly served in the military) states that when he 'saw these brave young lads on the news, telling us that they were "just doing their job", and that they were just going to "crack on", I am sorry to say I did not believe them. They were saying what was expected of them, what had been drilled into them, and I was sure they, and their stoically supportive families, did not fully understand what was really ahead.' In a significant moment at the start of *Casualties*, we encounter soldiers Gary and Mike on the night before their return to service in Afghanistan and the bomb disposal team. They strangely observe that Helmand province might actually be a more attractive proposition than their war-affected broken home life. We then cut to a riveting extended sequence of short intercut scenes where the parallel lives of Gary and Mike and their utterly bleak military existence is graphically and tragically exposed.

Acting notes

Peter's speech risks asking of its audience a sort of instant sympathy, as though emotion is easy and almost disposable. The actor must not wear the 'pity me' face, tortured by painful recollection, and he must not spoon out the horror of being blown-up and losing a limb for this would be the easy option, one that can be acted in ready-made heroic shorthand. We have seen it all before. For real horror to look at us directly, the man, not the hero, must be found and the largeness of theme should be reduced to the moment-by-moment reality of what is being said. To humanize such an effecting and difficult theme will require the smallest of thoughts that must cohere with other equally tiny points of reference. Through the cracks we will encounter this man's truth.

Peter   When you step on a pressure plate you think you hear the
click, or you think you feel it, but you don't know for sure. And you
can't know because what you remember … what you remember – well,
some of it isn't true. It isn't real. Your mind makes things up, gives you
false memories, tries to rationalise things, tries to join the dots. In my
head I am sure I knew it was going to happen, I knew I was going to
get myself blown up and I couldn't stop it. I couldn't change my fate.
But that can't be true, can it? Surely? I can't really have known, can I?
Because if I'd known, if I'd known, then how selfish of me was that?
Because when I stepped on that plate it didn't just screw up my life, it
screwed up the lives of all those people who ever cared for me, all those
people who ever loved me, all those people whose lives ever touched
mine. You see, in our pain we forget don't we, we forget about the
others. We are selfish in our suffering and we forget about the feelings
of others, about what they are going through, and we turn and stare at
that wall. In your pain I think you and Mike sought comfort in each
other's company. What happened is of no consequence because Mike
saw in it what he wanted, he hung onto that moment, and in the end it
was all he had. When he came back to you and you turned away from
him you took all that he had from him. There was nothing left back here
for him, and there was nothing out there for him.

City Love by Simon Vinnicombe

I feel like asking him to stay. To never leave this
room. But I know that son he will leave and ...

City Love received its world premiere at the CLF Art Café, Bussey Building,
Peckham Rye on 10 September 2013 and was directed by Sarah Bedi.

Context

Simon Vinnicombe's two-hander is remarkable in that it is an old-
fashioned boy-meets-girl romance but with contemporary issues.
Vinnicombe's characters play out storybook moments more typically
seen via Hollywood's vision of London in love – the breathless first
encounter that leads us through anticipation, passion and joy to the inevitable everyday problems that can all too easily fracture and destroy a
relationship. The play presents a sequence of sometimes heart-wrenching
extended monologues.

Acting notes

The acting challenge is quite clear. Such storytelling certainly requires a
performance style that doesn't inadvertently collapse into the easy cliché
of *Four Weddings and a Funeral* textbook 'rom-com' method – all sighs
and sad looks. Lovers and loving are often played as simple truths. The
trap for any actor is not to accidentally play character with a single focus
or straight-lined inner life, one that is just in or out of love. How will
the dishes get washed or the bills get paid? How will the inner joys of
partnership be met alongside the nagging doubts of union? Presenting
young love as dramatic subject matter is potentially quite dull to watch,
for it is actually a quite ordinary (and lovely) experience. Finding the
tension between inner doubts, fears and confusions alongside the blind
overwhelming experience of loving and being loved is the challenge.
The staging of the original production was very simple, with the actors
perched on separate boxes, only to meet in the middle when in love and
to separate once more when out of it. This simplicity should give a clear
sense of performance style but it does not give immediate solutions to the
dreary danger of acting someone 'in lerv'. A strong dynamic inner world
of questions and doubts will need to be constructed.

The second speech, much later in the play, taps into this darker aspect. Jim betrays Lucy. Though confessional in tone, there is the sense that his words are uttered by way of justification. The first text, first kiss and first moment of sex are all listed without passion or joy. The overarching sense is that of Jim's regret as opposed to his excitement ('we say nothing the entire way home'). The outer actions of his affair (touching or kissing) are counterbalanced by his inner despair.

Contemporary London, mid-twenties

Jim   I think my teeth got stuck on my lips when I tried to smile. Always happens when I'm nervous.

So I don't want to smile.

When I do it's a half of one. Sort of. Half leering. Half. Moron.

Can't work out if she's looking at me or looking where the bus is going. She fiddles with the back of a hair in her finger and thumb. Looks like she's thinking about something else. Someone else.

Girls like confidence, don't they?

I feel hot. Bit sweaty. Not in a sexy way. Wow.

Fuck me. She's so pretty. Oh my God, she's just …

Why is it that every time I try and look cool I just come across as a complete prick?

For the first minute or so I'm okay at not talking. But then it becomes a failure.

I'm bottling it again.

What's the worst that can happen?

… She gets off the bus.

Lucy *goes.*

Jim   And she's gone.

I look around the bus and *everyone* else knows. Even the driver knows.

That I am an apology for a human being.

Back to my hole in the city where no one can see me. Back to non-living. Back to …

No.

At the next stop …

I get off the bus. And I run back towards the previous stop. I'm overcome with a sense to see her again.

Which almost vanishes as I get close.

He is looking at **Lucy** *sitting at a bus stop.*

Jim   She's sat there. With her arms crossed, waiting for another bus. The light from the shelter shines down on her cheeks. Those eyes. Her hair. Her tights-clad legs crossed over one another as she sits. So perfectly. So. Wow.

I suddenly get a feeling that she's far too good for me.

I've got no right talking to her. I don't have any words to say.

Contemporary London, mid-twenties

Jim   I sleep with another girl that night. I sleep with Kim. The betrayal was there the first text I sent her.

I tell her I'm in her area. Which is the first lie.

From the minute we meet I can tell she is dressed up. For me. She looks right into my eyes. And then just below. And then into my eyes.

I'm flattered and excited.

I'd like to tell you that I don't think of Lucy during any of it. That I drank too much and one thing led to another and things just happened. But they don't. And they didn't.

The decision to kiss her takes over an hour. The thought begins when we're sat at the bar. She rests her hand on my thigh as she laughs. I think of kissing her. I think of Lucy.

Lucy *sits alone on the bed. She checks her watch.*

Jim   She likes my stories. Laughs at them. And it feels so good.

Lucy *tries to distract herself. She puts some music on.*

Jim   And neither of us want the night to end.

So we go on. We ignore the bouncers itching for an excuse to fight in the nightclub with no sign on the door. And the bar staff who hate you on sight. And the DJ posing as a cool bloke but in reality is a sex pest in his mid-thirties who lives with his mum.

The sex pest is playing PM Dawn. 'How have people become nostalgic for shit?' she says.

I smile and nod as if she's said the most funny and profound thing all at once. I'm already looking at her and wondering what her breasts look like without the clothes covering them.

And talking to her is so easy. It always is when you don't care. She takes my hand when the lights come up and the club

spills out. And we say nothing the entire way home. Perhaps if

we stay silent then it will be like we've done nothing wrong.

I think of Lucy all the way to her flat in that taxi. I think of her waiting for me. And I try to get angry at her to justify …

I have sex with her. I have sex with Kim.

The Cow Play by Ed Harris

The tail will grow to be twenty-four inches long.
At least. Fully grown, it might be anywhere between twenty-four
and forty-eight inches long.

The Cow Play was originally commissioned by Squaremoon Ltd in 2005.
This new version by Smoke & Oakum previewed at Theatre503 before
transferring to the Edinburgh Festival in 2013.

Context

Quite simply, a young woman is turning into an animal – a cow. This
disturbing idea is presented in a deceptively simple mix of both night-
marish and at times near farcical ordinariness. The play is not what it
might seem though, for as well as the bovine problem, there also seems
to be something far less extraordinary but no less difficult to deal with –
depression. The difficulties of such physical and mental torment take their
toll on Holly and her musician boyfriend. In his published introduction
to the play, Ed Harris writes that 'I wanted to explore some of the effects
that a typically "hidden" compulsion or psychological illness can have
on a relationship. I chose cows because of the etymological roots of
one such illness, but more importantly because of a cow's nature. Cows
have a kind of elegance and serenity, and in the same breath, they're
relatively unintelligible emotionally, giving them a sort of emptiness.' The
following speech is a sort of epilogue to the play, it could be spoken by
Owen, Holly's boyfriend.

Acting notes

This is a brutally honest speech. Ugly and beautiful. For it to maintain its
impact it should not veer to the sentimental or have a sort of gushing past
tense rhythm of a time long, long ago. The struggle within the mind of
the actor should be focused on what might have happened if the character
Owen had been there to answer Holly's call, what might have happened
if he hadn't ended their relationship. Is this reflective speech a slow realization of guilt or is it the piece-by-piece formation of one's life moving
on from something truly awful? The actor should note the presentation of
the text. It becomes more like a graphic score on the lines 'I'm hurting',

representing perhaps the intended thinking rhythm of the moment. The space between what is said and what is remembered.

Twenties – Early thirties

Owen   She wrote poems
That wouldn't be published till she was dead.
'Like Marilyn Monroe,' she said. And on those long
Militantly cold winter evenings, she'd ring
And tell me how sad she was, which was sad.
Or how she wanted my cock in her mouth,
'I want you to cum over my tits,' she said.
And she'd masturbate, or pretend to,
Until she made herself climax.
She was a tiny thing calling, from a faraway place.

I miss you, I'd say. And she'd tell me not to pressure her,
And usually go quiet and fall asleep, still on the phone.
Sometimes she would tell me she was in love with me,
And then not to pressure her.

One night she rang, and I was with others,
So I didn't answer. That night I missed the call.
I was her one call, she said later, there was no one else.
She spent the night in hospital (I can't remember
Whether a stomach pump was necessary)
And was released the next day.

So I stayed on the phone to her all the next few weeks.
I'd missed one call and wasn't going to miss another,
(Said our hero, weather-beaten, through gritted teeth
Standing up against the slamming, shining winter
That broke the backs of horses and felled trees.)
'I wish you were here to look after me,' she said,
A tiny something-cub calling over the phone.
'Do you love me more than [fill in the blank]?'
I do, I said. 'What about [x + y]?' I do, I said,
And she told me not to pressure her.

In the end, even I began to see a pattern forming.
Extracting myself took cold, lonely strength.
Because still she'd call out to me in my
Yearning, longing yearlong return:
Only occasionally, it's true, but clearly,
Out of the tundra behind me,
Calling: I miss you,
            I'm hurting,
                  I love you,

And I'd picture some small, trapped thing
Caught in a bear trap,
Slathered in slamming, shining snow.
The tiny something-cub calling
Its possibly last call, calling
Its one call,
          there is no one else.

The Effect by Lucy Prebble

I can tell the difference between who
I am and a side effect.

The Effect was co-produced by Headlong and the National Theatre and received its world premiere at the National Theatre's Cottesloe Theatre on 6 November 2012. It was directed by Rupert Goold.

Context

Two pharmaceutical drugs trial volunteers, Tristan and Connie, consent to being given ever larger doses of as yet untested new drugs. Two doctors monitor the effect. The volunteers suffer from another even more potent reaction – love – but are not sure if it is real or a toxic result of dopamine. The doctors argue about whether what has happened is chemically induced and, therefore, something that can be treated by other drugs, or something real and unprompted. Technically, the playwright finds tidy symmetry between the lives of both the medical and volunteer couples. They seem, at points, to blur into a combined larger universal experiment that questions not only the efficacy of drugs and the pharmaceutical industry, but also identity, truth and the power and majesty of human love.

Acting notes

This speech is a medical doctor giving a lecture. Facts upon facts. How many of us have stared at an authority figure like Dr Toby Sealey and wondered what is really going on in his head? What thoughts is he having as the narration continues to be spoken? When approaching this speech it should be remembered that the facts are the least important aspect of the performance. More important is the psychology of the man behind them. The task for the actor is to track down the clues that betray his inner thinking landscape. In this speech, he actually reveals very little of himself: there are no momentary slips; no references to his personal life; his dreams, fears or passions. This professional flatness reveals a sort of professionalism and education, and the fact that he has probably given this lecture many times before for it is well prepared and, in delivery terms, very smooth. Additionally, the loss of self (and the more usual personal pronoun 'I') for the more collective 'we' of the medical establishment indicates how he identifies himself with that establishment. Does he aspire to this blanket professional anonymity or is he already part of it? Much later in the play, Toby confesses to his medical colleague that he loves her, but that 'It's not romantic cos that's when lies start.' Is he holding all his emotion in, keeping himself under wraps, losing himself in his professional self for some reason? What is this reason?

Forty-five years, 91kg, 188cm

Toby   When the brain goes wrong, there are symptoms and there
are physical causes, as with anything else. But because we *think* with
our brain we struggle to frame it as the complex piece of biological
machinery it is. We're happy to have heart transplants and liver
transplants but we can't imagine a brain transplant. Because nowadays
we think our soul is in there. But that sense of 'us' is only a small part
of what's going on at any moment. As you sit listening to me your brain
is generously taking care of the basics to keep you alive; breathing, your
heart pumping. But it's also regulating other things so you don't have to
be consciously aware of them, your temperature, ignoring the sound of
other people breathing, forcing food through your gut, positioning your
spinal column in your seat, which doesn't look terribly comfortable, I'm
sorry. Swallowing so you don't choke on your saliva. Actively thinking
about these things doesn't help but the brain is taking care of it. And
if we suffered a neurological oddity that meant we couldn't swallow
we'd see nothing wrong with addressing and repairing that in the brain.
There are diseases of the brain. Since we've been able to begin scanning
and mapping the brain in the last quarter century we're much closer to
understanding its functions and its malfunctions. And rather than have
people feel they're crazy or incapable or dangerous in soul, we're able
to show them what they really are. Ill. We need to consider mental
health the same way we do the bodily kind, because it is the bodily kind.

Even Stillness Breathes Softly Against a Brick Wall by Brad Birch

I wonder what people care about in a war zone.
I wonder in what ways their problems change.
Yes you're fighting for your life
but what about your bills?

Even Stillness Breathes Softly Against a Brick Wall was first performed at the Soho Theatre Upstairs, London, on 28 May 2013, directed by Nadia Latif and produced by Tabula Rasa Theatre.

Context

In his introduction to the play, Brad Birch reveals that *Even Stillness* started life as a poem about a couple (a nameless 'Him' and 'Her'), who were becoming disheartened with the 'trammels of the modern world'. Their voices, he suggests, 'began to fight back', rejecting the misery and humdrum their lives were subjected to. Birch is interested in the point at which we become 'Frankenstein constructs, where what we are is amended and augmented by what've consumed'. The play's claustrophobic landscape 'within a small flat' is inhabited by two nameless people who quite literally 'appear'. Their opening words are an echoed refrain of 'wake up, wake up', as much a call to arms as a morning's evocation. Indeed, much of the dialogue throughout the play feels like it should be spoken with a sort of distant Brechtian remove for, no matter who speaks, exchanges mostly begin with the personal pronoun 'I'. The characters actually talk of very ordinary domestic things such as the struggle of getting up for work in the morning or even just making a cup of tea. But such domestic matters are gradually overwhelmed by an eerily-constructed social, moral and personal collapse. The play's impending sense of near-animal-revolt against hated consumer capitalism is, in the final moments, strangely poetical as well as clearly political. 'Him' and 'Her' finally confront the dire context of their powerless situation with an act of utter rebellion.

Acting notes

The namelessness of the character 'Him' is a useful key route to performance but it could be misread as a do-nothing-much-in-particular type of clause. This character could be anyone – *is anyone* – but the fact is that to perform it well 'He' must be invested with very recognizable definition (if he is not to be presented in a flat or empty way). While he is seemingly anonymous, we learn about his parents, the current situation of war, local anarchy, fires in Geneva, families being murdered in Spain, a debt crisis throwing millions into chaos, and so on. We are given a lot of information which requires some sort of emotional and intellectual engagement and alignment or it will just assume the flatness of a sequence of facts. How does 'He' feel about each of these strange and terrifying occurrences? His references to family, and in particular his dad, make it impossible to just talk about family as a remote construct without any other memories seeping into what is being said. The actor playing this role will therefore have to construct owned and personal meanings which are far from nameless. We the audience must have a sense of this man's life and experience, his hopes, dreams and fears. How is he coping in these extreme times? Namelessness is not the same as having no inner life or intention. Is 'He' part of the revolution? The namelessness a mere cover for something far more sinister.

Him   First I thought she'd fucked up.
I mean I know I leave it to her
but we work and that should be enough.
If you work then you should be able to afford to …
I mean yeah, I've had to lend my parents a few quid
but you can afford that.
You should be able to afford that.

My dad calls with good news.
He's got a job.
I ask him what doing.
It's picking litter in a park.

You can just imagine him there.
These little shits.
Little bastards dropping rubbish everywhere.
And there's my dad behind
picking up after them.
If they shat on the pavement
would he have to pick that up too?

The war today spread
to the neighbouring provinces.
The civil outbreak has caused
the international community
to condemn the people for fighting for their lives.
They've never seen fire in Geneva.

I read an article online
about a Spaniard who shot himself and his family.

They say he was deranged.
Say he had issues.

Though the reasons he shot himself they report
were mounting debts, the loss of his job
troubles with alcohol dependency
and pressures at home.

Now that to me doesn't sound like derangement.
To me that sounds like
the whole fucking world falling in on him.

The Grand Gesture adapted by Deborah McAndrew from *The Suicide* by Nikolai Erdman

Up to this very moment I've been nothing
more than a national insurance number,
a statistic – the sum of boxes ticked on
a social security form.

The Grand Gesture was originally produced by Northern Broadsides in partnership with Harrogate Theatre and given its world premiere on 6 September 2013 at Harrogate Theatre. It was directed by Conrad Nelson.

Context

It was Vsevolod Meyerhold who created the 'great' now historical stagings of Erdman's farcical and delightfully grotesque play *The Suicide*. In this adaptation, Semyon, now Simeon, is the suicidally-inclined anti-hero. A difficult subject for comedy, even when adapted as it is here by Deborah McAndrew, who transports 1920s Russia to the dingy boarding house world of the north-west of England. Simeon (living off his wife's meagre wages) announces that he is fed up with the pointlessness of it all and is therefore going to kill himself, not convinced of any real reason for carrying on. The news is greeted by a stream of grotesque visitors to the soon-to-be dead man. They are vultures who see his death as an opportunity for gain, however small. But as the farewell preparations progress, Simeon notices the most simple and beautiful things about the life he will soon extinguish.

Acting notes

Like a suicide note, this speech contains within it all the clues to the personality and poor state of mind of Simeon. But it is a constructed mind too, not all chaos and tearful despair. A mind that quotes *Macbeth* Act 5, scene 5 ('Tomorrow, and tomorrow, and tomorrow. Creeps in this petty pace from day to day'). While Macbeth considers the 'way to dusty death', Simeon is left wondering the exactness of the trigger-pulled moment. How the bullet leaves the gun and at what point the victim crosses the 'void'. There is something incredibly rational, ordered and methodical; possibly the tidiness of a life in completion. Or is this the language and thinking pattern of a man digressing from his once clear intent? It feels ponderous, overly analysed and rather like a self-dramatization of a pitiful moment, not the pitiful moment itself. The actor can play this speech as a preamble to death itself or, remarkably, the preamble to life. The character's inner thinking landscape will need careful attention and preparation, for this is not actually a speech to demonstrate or show an over emotive state – all tears and screaming – but rather an opportunity for the actor to inhabit a mind in free fall.

Simeon   Tomorrow. Tomorrow. Tomorrow.

I guess we've all gotta go sometime. If I didn't die yesterday, and I don't die today, I'll surely die tomorrow. Blimey – I feel as old as the universe – from end to end. All of time … time … What does that mean?

You hold a gun to your head and time passes, a second – a tick of the clock – and another – tock. But between the tick and the tock there's this void to cross. A quantum leap has to be made between the tick and the tock and if you don't make it … Tick – a man is a man. Tock – a man is no more. Nothing.

And the trigger of the gun – that's the key isn't it: the key that opens the void. You flick the safety catch – click. You squeeze the trigger – bang! Click – a man is a man. Bang – a man is no more.

Now – I've got a fair idea about the tick and the click … but the tock and the bang? 'Tick and click' is here, now, lodgings, wife, mother-in-law, ten fingers, ten toes, sun, sky, scrap heap. But what's 'tock and bang', eh? It's none of those things, and I can't imagine that … no lodgings, no wife, no mother-in-law (well, maybe I could stretch to imagining that) but you get my drift. Nothing. No Simeon Duff.

And what's Simeon Duff anyway? A man. What is a man? A piece of work? A temple of the soul – is that it? And when the temple is torn down what happens to the soul? Does it fly around like a burst balloon? And is it glad to be free of all the suffering in the world? Are the pearly gates shining? Does Saint Peter see you and say, 'come on, lad, your troubles are over – from now on it's egg flip all the way'? Will I fall asleep in the arms of Jesus? Or is it all – just – nothing …

Three **Gypsies** *enter – carrying clocks.*

And is nothing any worse than this?

The clocks chime the hour.

Hidden in the Sand by James Phillips

I think we've been waiting for each other
And so I'm going to trust you. That's all
you can do with people. Say this is my
heart and if you drop it then it will break.

Hidden in the Sand received its world premiere on 1 October 2013 at the Trafalgar Studios, London. It was directed by the writer, James Phillips.

Context

A beautiful Greek Cypriot refugee, Alexandra, living in London and running a modest jewellery store, is seduced one night by middle-aged Jonathan, an awkward but charming English classical scholar. He studies an unknown classical past whereas she is trying to forget hers. Can such an accidental coupling result in more than just a clumsy one-night stand? Alexandra must confront the memories of her life before London, which are firmly locked away, stored like a painful set of secrets in a jewellery box. Jonathan, too, must learn to deal with the historical past in a new way if he is ever going to have a future with this beautiful, but troubled, woman. James Phillips's play is a haunting evocation of love at its most simple and true, but it is also a ghost story where the facts of the past have to be re-imagined and thought through anew. Its poetic, intimate, almost dreamy literary style is offset by an eerie ever-present feeling that every encounter we have in life is totally out of our control. The two monologues selected from this play are from very different points in Jonathan's relationship with Alexandra.

Acting notes

In performance terms at least, passion should never be played as a generic catch-all emotion but rather, a driven, exquisite experience informed by very personal detail, often so forensically harvested that its formation defies logic. Passion is an impulse informed by something, not just itself. In the first speech, Jonathan is absolutely overwhelmed by Alexandra; the emotional vertigo Jonathan feels is brilliantly given voice. But what exactly is Jonathan's real intention, moment by moment? Is he using charming phrases as a form of clever (if not rather deceitful) form entrapment? A wordy way to convince Alexandra that she should have sex with him? Is this part of his well-rehearsed, all blushing and awkward patter? Why is it difficult for him to articulate how and what he feels? His first line: 'Can I touch you?' is very direct indeed. Is the rest of the speech a retreat from such directness, a cover-up for having revealed too much? Is it sex that will bring him happiness or the possibility of long-term companionship?

In the second speech it is as though a completely different man is speaking to the same woman. Things have changed. Is this the real Jonathan speaking, devoid of flirty classical references and presumed innocence? The two speeches seen together offer the actor a very useful insight into the character's emotional dimension – not a 'before' and 'after' as such, but certainly differing qualities which will need to cohere. Both share a core and almost alarming sense of honesty.

A classical scholar at Oxford University, forties

Jonathan   Can I touch you?

Neither of them moves.

Jonathan   I didn't mean to say it like that. I was decisive, once.

I don't remember how this is done. I didn't used to be this sort of person I don't think. I think we get altered, as we get older, by events.

He has natural charm but an often covered and deep shyness, although I don't know if he'd recognise this about himself.

The woman is watching. She has straight hair, black, loose around her face. Small, slender, angles in her face, slight of build. Strikingly beautiful, but her looks are an irrelevance to her. Something slightly bohemian in her dress sense, we will notice perhaps.

He moves towards her, reaches out his hand, touches her gently. Everything in the room about their physical proximity, her body and its geography.

Jonathan   In the cab I was thinking about this moment. I was trying to look like I was thinking about something else but that's what I was thinking about. That's why I kept looking out the window. I was thinking about the practicalities of holding your hand.

So I started to think about what Aphrodite might have advised in this situation. But the scholar runs into problems there you see. Because there are layers of myth, there are these different Aphrodites. Difficult thing, love.

He has not moved his hand, forward or back: sensual impasse. She has smiled.

She had no childhood: she was born fully formed. That'd make a person confident. Or oblivious. But you probably know this, because Aphrodite's a Cypriot like you are. If the myths are to be believed.

She leans slightly towards him, testing the motion.

I talk too much. Once I gave my godson a twelve-minute diatribe about the variety and antics of talking trees in classical myth. He was three. He was waiting to open his presents. He was very polite about it.

This is very possibly the worst seduction ever undertaken in pre- or post-classical human history. I do know that.

I didn't expect to come back. (*simply*) I like you so much.

A classical scholar at Oxford University, forties

Jonathan (*deep feeling*) – I don't understand love at all, I don't understand it, but all I know, all I have learnt is that it is not what I thought it was, and that it can change. My wife taught me that.

That it is skimming a stone across an ocean, trying to reach someone.

And I know that I want to leave the room with you, and that is the entire field of enquiry here. That is the whole fucking world. After that you can hold my hand or not.

I know that when I was young I had pride and that now I have no pride but more strength and I don't know whether your husband is alive or dead, or whether you will find him if he is alive or if he would want to be found. But I do know

that I want to leave the room with you. And I do know that if we don't speak out loud to the people we care about, speak out loud every day, then we will die. I think we have been dying inside, you and I, and we should stop.

I am alone, a lot, for my work and because of things that have happened to me. I speak stupidly. I don't know how to do this, to make someone like you. I don't know how to

trust you, but somehow I have trusted you every minute since the first time I looked across that little shop and said

'Amos-chostos'.

A History of Falling Things by James Graham

I just. Wanted to tell stories. Loved them
growing up. Even though they generally scared the shit out
of me. Think children's stories can be the scariest of all.

A History of Falling Things was first performed at Clwyd Theatre, Mold, on 23 April 2009. It was directed by Kate Wasserberg.

Context

The play is a romantic almost sentimental comedy about fear, or more precisely, irrational fear including the fear of falling things: shoes, satellites and almost anything. Robin and Jacqui are virtually neighbours and most significantly, virtual lovers, who only meet online because they both possess such fears. In his introduction, playwright James Graham describes how the play is 'essentially a relationship drama' and that 'many of Robin's annoying, irrational anxieties' resemble his own. The play is brilliantly crafted with dream-like sequences that are both funny and achingly sad in the same moment. The fears are overwhelming and life is clearly passing both Robin and Jacqui by as we see their bewildered worlds diminish.

Acting notes

Like many of the characters in James Graham's plays, their ordinariness should not be seen as being in any way simple. In *A History of Falling Things*, the character Robin is seemingly just an average sort of guy who has an unfortunate habit of finding normal things a little scary. In this first speech, Robin recounts a long list of things that have fallen out of the sky, things that have either hurt or killed people. The list is impressive and appears to be historically researched, containing many facts, but are these actually facts? As Robin describes each new extraordinary episode, there is a sense that he might just be manufacturing completely irrational or imagined stories to explain or justify his fears. The long stream of information would be overwhelming in an ordinary social context, but its excess has a dream-like quality, removing it from the real. At different points in the speech it rains frogs, fish, coins and even blood. Robin is unwell; his mind is clogged up with so many fears as to render him incapable of sound judgement. His reality has become distorted but to him it is very real.

In the second speech, we learn of when Robin's father died. This is a very moving account of the moment when, unable to leave his house due to the fear of falling things, Robin has to watch as his family and his father's funeral hearse pull away from their house. After the funeral, his brother Mark punches him in the stomach. All the necessary information for a truthful performance is usefully given by the playwright. The actor must decide whether Robin has been in some way damaged by this moment or is merely reflecting upon it. At the end of the speech he states that he has not spoken properly with his brother since the funeral and that he doesn't think that that is fair. It would appear that all is not resolved or forgiven between them. Robin is a man; it is for the actor to decide whether he can build an informed and new life from such reflection.

Robin   Cats and dogs. From what I can tell it has never ever rained cats and dogs anywhere. What has been recorded though is frogs ...

It starts to rain frogs.

Lots and lots of frogs. Above Minneapolis in 1901, a green cloud appeared overhead, and a deluge began. While driving through Scotland in 1955, falling frogs pelted Nellie Straw's car. They fell again as recently as 1981 in Nephalion, Greece, where frogs, at the time, were not even indigenous. They are now. The only hypothesis the scientists can cling to is the waterspout phenomenon, where animals are sucked up into the sky and carried through clouds before being dropped over land. Then there's the fish.

It starts to rain fish.

Some perch fish showered a parking lot in Northern Australia, some four hundred miles from the sea. Catfish, bream and bass rained down over Alabama in 1956. Local legend records that they were very, very tasty.

It starts to rain notes, and then coins.

Lucky were a French community in 1957 when thousand-franc notes floated down over their village from a clear blue sky. Less lucky, depending on how you look at it, were the party of schoolchildren being walked home in Manchester, 1982, when they began to be pelted with pennies. The more resourceful ones not injured gathered as much as they could and ran straight to the nearest sweet shop. Stranger still, the coins that fell over Gorky in Russia were from the sixteenth century and could not be accounted for.

Various objects now begin to rain down.

The house in Evans, Colorado, that for the past one hundred and twenty odd years has suffered the occasional shower of corn, battering its roof. Then there is the as yet unproven myth of the Japanese fishing boat sunk off the coast of Siberia – the traumatised crew insisting wholeheartedly that the hole in the middle of the deck was caused by nothing other than ... a cow. Falling from above.

It begins to rain blood.

And in Li Yan, France, and in Calabria, Italy, and in California, and in India, where recorded, falling from the sky, were tiny little droplets of scarlet red blood ...

Robin   It was. When my dad died. And it was his funeral. And I got to the end of the path, through the gate. Uh. Under the big tree by my road. It was pissing it down.

He enters the centre space. Under a tree. Rain and thunder. He holds himself tight.

Everyone was waiting in the cars. Mum. My brother, Mark. They, they'd tried to make it as easy as possible for me. The whole procession, pulling right up to my house. All I had to do was run across the road and get in. But then once I'm in the car, what then? Start screaming, have a panic attack? Mark and Mum had got sick of tugging on me, getting wet. Now they're just sat in the front car. Faces appearing intermittently between the sweeps of the windscreen wipers. Imploring me just to come that little bit further. But I can't. Looking at the hearse. 'Dad', written in flowers. I want to so much. So much. But I can't. My brother's face. I was ruining everything. But I'd gone as far as I could. So I turned around, and walked back inside.

He re-enters his house. Sits. Silence.

When they came back, my mum went next door to say thank you for something or other. I asked Mark how it had gone, and he said, 'Fine.' And then he hit me in the stomach. And it hurt. And I deserved it. But then as I was trying to stand he hit me again. And I didn't think I deserved that. I was the one who had missed the funeral and I'd missed it because it was becoming about me and I didn't want it to be about me, it was meant to be about Dad, and I couldn't understand why he couldn't understand that. I had wanted to go and stand up and talk about him. About the way he would do some proper old- school whistling as he mowed the lawn and the way he would drum with a fork on the biscuit tin; I'd wanted to do that. Mark went on about funerals being for the living, not the dead. And that day had been for Mum. And I had let her down. We haven't really spoken since; not properly. And I don't think that's fair.

If You Don't Let Us Dream, We Won't Let You Sleep By Anders Lustgarten

I don't know what you're afraid of
but I know what it looks like.
I was married to fear most of my life
Don't give in to it.

If You Don't Let Us Dream, We Won't Let You Sleep received its world premiere at the Royal Court Theatre, London, on 15 February 2013 and was directed by Simon Godwin.

Context

According to the playwright Anders Lustgarten, this satire was written 'for the return of political theatre' and to help people understand the 'killer zombie' of austerity. By its own logic, the free market model is dead, killed when it required huge bailouts of public money that violate its key tenet of operating without state support. Yet, restored to life by our cash, neo-liberalism lumbers on, chomping our vital services. Lustgarten describes how people have been turned off conventional politics because they believe that it makes absolutely no difference, and are starting to take politics into their own hands in a variety of ways. He sees this play not as old-style agit-prop but 'anti-prop', populated by government officials, business representatives and politicos working to targets and developing cost-effective plans that will 'monetize' the poor and give the investor a good return. We also meet disaffected teachers, nurses and a group of dissidents who attempt to establish a Court of Public Opinion in which the reasons and creators of economic austerity will be put on trial.

Acting notes

Playing any character that partly represents a political idea is difficult in the context of a monologue or speech for audition because the performance can become overwhelmed by the logic of the argument and it can therefore appear more like a spoken manifesto rather than a living voice and presence. This has always been the challenge of political theatre by George Bernard Shaw or Bertolt Brecht. This play's original setting was without concrete location and was performed 'without decor'. A multitude of interchangeable characters were, by their sheer critical mass, seemingly anonymous, named only by their trade (workman, nurse, administrator) and seemed to exist in the moment of an immediate idea as opposed to as a sum of their lives. Therefore, be cautious – to play a 'workman' is to play no man at all. People are not defined by generic labels, but by their action or inaction, though, within that, the characters in this play are nevertheless also driven by feelings and desires. Here, a character with a real name, Tom, confesses something close to his heart. Tom is a rounded character set in the context of this fast-paced, short, intercut play, and his speech is almost like an operatic aria, rich with interior thoughts carefully revealed.

Ray (the character in the second monologue from this play) is a young Irish activist who seems to carry the weight of history on his shoulders. Although his words betray intelligence, passion and the confident political rhetoric of someone 'on' agenda and preoccupied with current social matters, what is interesting is the very personal clues he lets slip about his own background ('the church door', 'every family of four'). His past has affected him, but as he says later in the play, he didn't 'join a revolutionary autonomist organisation to sit in fucking meetings'.

Late twenties – Early thirties

Tom   Look, I don't … At the risk of sounding like a patronising ex-banker: I don't know if you really understand what you're dealing with. I live in a block of flats in Bow, and from my balcony you can see the City, squatting like a spider atop the town, daring anyone to take it on. And when you're in there, that's how you feel: where the fuck else would you want to be? I did an internship before my last year at uni, I'd never given a thought to finance before, but when you walk in, you're just like, 'Holy fuck. I want to work here.' Miles and miles of chrome and glass and a billion flickering numbers that pile up around you like snowdrifts … And you can press a button and change the value of the currency in Argentina. Press another one and a thousand people in Mumbai lose their jobs. Do you have any idea how good that feels? How seductive it is to know that people know you can do that to them, and are afraid of you? And even when you don't understand one fucking word of what is going on, Exhibit A, the derivatives market, which is why we had the financial crisis and are going to have another one, the outside world doesn't know that. Or have any idea how to change it. Do you really think you're going to stop all that, change the real rulers of this country, the system that keeps politicians on their knees, with (*gestures round the room*) this?

Irish political activist, twenties

Ray   D'you know what the worst of Ireland is, Jen? It's not the joblessness. Nor the rake of never-to-be-finished houses looming over you like scaffolds. It's the guilt. The giving in and the guilt. Ireland was bankrupted by fifteen men. There's fifteen property speculators owe Anglo Irish half a billion apiece and all the rest of us'll be choking on that for life and nobody says a thing because, for some literally insane reason, *we* feel guilty. Like somehow it's *our* fault we got robbed, because we had the temerity to want a little happiness. We had something beyond the cold creak of the church door, just for a moment, and then the greatest theft since Cromwell, and now every family of four is carrying two hundred thousand euros of someone else's debt and how in God's name are they supposed to pay it? There's a loss of life, a whole world of what could have been that's being strangled and *nobody will fight back*, and I'm as committed to this thing as anyone but if you think I'm going to say a single word in defence of those murderers you'd better think again, long and hard.

Joe Guy by Roy Williams

I do believe! The world is mine! You see, it's the look,
it's the look we all have when we see summin we want,
summin where you know it will mad you up if you see
someone else wid it, you know. And you say to your self, no,
nosir, nant have that. So you get down, as far as you can go,
then you go down some more.

Joe Guy had its world premiere at the New Wolsey Theatre, Ipswich, on 18 October 2007 and was directed by Femi Elufowoju, Jr.

Context

In *Joe Guy*, Roy Williams skilfully explores some difficult questions about community and its mythical place in Prime Minister, Tony Blair's Britain. Williams asks at what point does socio-cultural difference actually become a form of racism? The play's brilliance is that it never assumes the polemical extremes of a party political pamphlet, but rather, presents a wonderfully compelling, sometimes funny story of a young Ghanaian footballer who rises from Sunday League to the moneyed excesses of the Premier League. Joseph has such talent but is cursed with a sort of hard-wired inferiority in spite of his success. Shockingly, Joe feels just 'too black' and decides to change, not the colour of his skin but his identity, and in so doing becomes a 'yardie' and a newly formed cliché whose beating heart is desperately given away to whatever or whoever might be wanting it. We experience a newly constructed parody of the brilliant young man that was Joe, a rising star, who at the same time is ever more vulnerable and lonely.

Acting notes

The speech is complex in that it is a comic-turn, requiring the quick-fire selection of changing voices, but it is also an utterly believable demonstration of the long held frustrations and tensions of contemporary life. The character, Joe, is required to transform in front of our eyes, as we are taken on a whirlwind tour of the streets and the people on them. While an actor might relish the opportunity to show a range of performance skills, the speech is not just about showing-off; its performance requires a clear personal through-line marking each moment-by-moment decision. Why would anyone choose to radically change who they are? What extraordinary circumstances would push someone to actually become another person? Playwright Roy Williams brilliantly humanizes the political and social dilemma, but in this speech the actor is charged with getting inside the personal journey which is not entertaining but devastating.

Joe *is alone on stage. He faces the audience.*

Joe   'Yes, Joe, what up, blood!' No –

He tries again, but struggles to overcome his Ghanaian accent.

'Joe, my man, what you say, bruv' – not bruv, bro, say bro! 'Joe, my man, wass up, bruv.' Bro, not bruv! 'Wass up, blood.' 'Blood, man, blood, you get me, seen?' Yes, yes, Joseph, no, no, Joe, Joe Guy, me name's Joe Guy. Yes, blood, yes, man, yes! 'Wass up, blood, blood, blood, blood, blood, blood! Wasss up, blood!' (*Jubilant.*) Yes! Oh, yes! 'Wass up, blood! You awright, yeah, man! You know what I'm sayin', you get me yeah, gal fine man, she buff and she move her batty like, yeah, man, me safe, you cool, dread, me cool, man, nuff respect to yer, bruv, me down wid yer, you hear me, me down. Watch me fly now, you see! Me look cris, yes! Hey, yungsta, ware you go? You cool? Me cool, man! Oh man, that is heavy, you go 'low dat! Oh my daze! See how he reach for me, nuff times, you hear what I'm saying, you get me, seen! Kiss me neck back!'

His once strong Ghanaian accent is now fading.

'Move from me wid yer batty hole, Marcus, and yer stink breath, move, step! Is who you looking at? You scoping me? You want try summin? I don't see no one else here, Marcus, it's you one, looking at me! 'Bout you eyeballing me? You tink I go 'low dat, you dizzy or what? What do I look like to you, what do I sound like, some booboo big rubber-lips monkey-faced African bin bag? Dat ain't me no more, nosir! I'm oneyer you, I'm better dan you! I'm the new and improved model. Come now, dread, bring yerself, or is you a pussy? You pussy? I'll spark you in the fucking face, you nuh! From now until kingdom come, I go mash you up! Then I go sex yer woman, ca' she looking tit! Go ride her, bareback, Then I go dash it, and go laugh in yer face, tell you about yer batty hole! When I call, you best come, get me? Do you get me, Marcus! When I call, you come, that's the way it is now! That's the way it's gonna stay. I'm running things now – you get fresh, you get cut. You come reach for me now, I go school you now, you pussy hole, rass clart, boomba hole, batty bwoi! Seen? Aiiiiieeee! You is the African one now. Don't step up unless you gonna jump!' (*Pleased with himself.*) Yes, that's good.

The Kindness of Strangers by Curious Directive

You never forget your first shift. Sheets of
snow. In April. 1985. My son had just been born. I had to try
to save a baby just a few months older than him on my first
trip out. Nightmare.

The Kindness of Strangers was a co-production between Curious Directive
and the Norfolk & Norwich Festival. It was first performed in May 2013
and toured the UK in 2014. It was directed by Jack Lowe.

Context

The Kindness of Strangers began life in the back of an ambulance. In
director Jack Lowe's introduction to the play, he describes how his mother
told him a story about paramedics travelling from Norwich to London.
His research, with the company Curious Directive, led to many conversations with ambulance staff and those working in the NHS. The result of
his extensive research was not translated into a heart-rending stage play,
but an ushering of the audience into 'Old Rosie', a 1968 ambulance, and
a site-specific encounter with the voices and lives of the paramedic world.
And so five or so audience members at a time, each wearing earphones,
embark on an average night's work on the front line. We meet Sylvia on
her last shift and Lisa on her first. While on the imagined journey, the
ambulance doors are flung open on to different emergency scenarios.

Acting notes

In the play, we randomly encounter Ben. He just cycles up to us and gives
us his story, almost like a witness statement, and having done so, then
cycles off. His story has order, logic and design to it. Ben has a precise,
methodological nature. He enjoys study and is clearly absorbed by his
subject. What is of interest here is that in the context of the play, all this
order is utterly destroyed 'on the morning of the accident'. The acting
challenge is to authenticate the sense of this character's obvious intellect
and joy of learning, the rhythm of his daily routines and journeys. Why
does he so overly describe all this, when clearly in the foreground of his
thinking is the accident?

Late twenties

Ben   My subject is psychology.

I'm interested in how our surroundings influence our development; it's called Ecological Systems Theory. I also like thinking about the moments in which we reveal ourselves, and suddenly realise who we are. You need those moments to know that you're still a person.

I'm a lark. I mean, I'm up with them. Before them actually, sometimes.

If I'm in my office at seven, I don't have to drink the coffee that's been stewing for three hours and I don't have to make small-talk with students at the bike-racks. I find that weird – I'm ten years older than them and they treat me like their grandparents. You know, like a 'square'. I'm not a square.

I cycle to work because my route takes me straight through the heart of the city – you can't do that by car. Like drilling a hole through an onion. I get to see the best and worst of it, every morning.

Beat.

My work considers the individual as a product of nested environmental systems.

I'm sorry, that's obscure.

Have you ever seen a set of Russian dolls? You're the tiny one in the middle that can't be taken apart. And each *network*, if you like, exists outside of you at varying distances.

For example, the microsystem is the groups that most directly affect us: family, school, religious insitutions.

Then exosystem: our parents' friends, our friends' parents, their work, you know, outside of ourselves but touching us. Maybe your auntie in Australia's ill and you wonder why Dad's acting funny.

Then macro: our race, our culture, our wealth and circumstances. Whether you see people that look like you on the telly, or in government.

And chronosystem: that's basically the idea that sometimes an event that changed who we were at the time doesn't seem so bad a few years later.

These dolls knock together, passing sounds between themselves, with us at the centre.

Land of Our Fathers by Chris Urch

I can't believe we're arguing over a Blue Ribband
I can't believe we're stuck down a mine
Yet here we are.

Land of Our Fathers received its world premiere at Theatre503, London, on 18 September 2013 and was directed by Paul Robinson. It transferred to Trafalgar Studios in September 2014.

Context

Literary Manager, Steve Harper, writes in the published play text that playwright Chris Urch's characters are 'unforgettable' and cites the fact that eminent British political dramatist Howard Brenton pronounced Urch to be one of the 'promising future voices of theatre'. Praise indeed for this seemingly modest play set in South Wales during the 1979 general election, about six miners trapped underground in a coal mine after an electrical explosion. The men must inhabit a darkened, dangerous world, ever threatening, ever destructive, awaiting their hoped-for freedom. We experience the full dimension of the disaster through Bomber, the experienced miner, and Mostyn, a youngster new to the world of the dark. At different points in the play the men's terrible situation is tested to the limit. Time slowly passes and, as all available jokes have been told, Mostyn rather surprisingly cajoles his fellow miners into a hearty rendition of 'My Favorite Things' from *The Sound of Music*, and later a close-harmony version of 'Pretty Vacant' by the Sex Pistols. But all is certainly not cosy – the enforced bonhomie and famed miners' discipline breaks up like the ground above their heads; a world of fearful survival and solitude reigns, but for how long?

Acting notes

Exhausted, hungry and tired, Curly and his fellow workers have had to deal with many days' entrapment in a dark and dangerous place. Lacking sleep and profoundly lacking hope since the death among them of their friend and colleague, Bomber the old miner, they are all talked-out and any dreams of safe escape have faded. Curly is sick of being told everything will be all right and has spent the last few days trying to sleep away his imprisonment. He awakens from a nightmare, breathing heavily and speaking seemingly nonsensical bits of his dream and of his previous life above the ground. His speech needs to be carefully unpacked; some images described are clearly on the nightmare spectrum and some connected more closely to the real context of entrapment and his fear of fading survival. To play near madness or desperation is very difficult indeed. There are of course, clichés available in one's own theatre- or film-going memory, but what of our real encounter with other's stress or difficulty? What of our own? Do we ever really conform to 'off-the-shelf' behaviour? Similar traits might well be identifiable, but each of us has our own contributing story, encoded by real and experienced moments in life. Curly's monologue will depend on a sort of imaginative emotional forensic investment.

Curly   I walk into the Black Lion and the food's still steaming.
Cigarettes burning, pints of bitter flood the floor. *Zeplin* plays on the
wireless but no ones there to talk over it. I run outside to the chippie.
It's dead quiet other than this blue cat sitting in the window with giant
fucking whiskers and yellow eyes. She purrs a call to arms. Replicas,
no, clones strut through the chippie parading themselves. Sipping spilt
vinegar, rolling round in the salt getting fatter and fatter. So fat I break
their furry fucking necks in two. Blood sprays everywhere and they
multiply back to life. Their claws slice me open as I stumble out and
sprint like fuck to the corner shop. These colossal lions chasing me.
Faster now. Roaring. Faster. I turn a corner and then nothing … Silence
… I look up at the sky and for a second I think to myself 'has it always
been this close?' It feels so close I could touch it. Burst it. And I want
to. By God do I want to. Every nerve ending in my body feels the need
to but I know if I did the clouds would all burst into flames. And then
I see you. No. It's your shadow. Mocking me. Echo's my name. I dash
after it. There's shadows everywhere now. Orange shadows, purple,
indigo, violet. I try and tackle them to the ground but they slip from
my grasp. My hands are coated in oil. Got you! I jump through your
silhouette, falling through the abyss landing outside my front door. Bam.
That's odd. Why's the doorstep not polished? Milk bottles, lined up
untouched. I slowly walk through the hallway now. Walls covered with
moths. They're mating. Fucking the life out of each other then shitting
on the wallpaper. An army of slugs parade along the carpet and tons of
money spiders hang from the ceiling like tiny lightshades. I tread on
weeks worth of unopened post and bills. Postcards from Spain. We don't
know anyone from Spain?

A Life of Galileo by Bertolt Brecht, adapted by Mark Ravenhill

In the year sixteen hundred and nine
The light of science shone
In a modest house in Padua
As Galileo set out to prove
That the Sunnis fixed
And the earth is on the move

A Life of Galileo received its world premiere at the Swan Theatre, Stratford-upon-Avon, in a production by the RSC on 31 January 2013. It was directed by Roxana Silbert.

Context

Mark Ravenhill's wonderfully theatrical translation of what is generally considered to be one of Brecht's finest plays was given such life and brilliance by this much needed edit of the longer, lofty original, and by the relevant updating in the original RSC staging. In this new version, Galileo's radical vision – that the earth moves around the sun – seems to be a beautiful, as opposed to merely scientific or dangerous, idea. But his thesis will bring ruin to both his personal and professional life and, post-inquisition, instruments of torture, not science, will expose mortal not celestial truths. *Galileo* is not a play about science but about the rapture of knowledge and its power for both good and bad.

Acting notes

Here we have a 'eureka' vision of our solar system. But Galileo is also aware of how this contravenes Vatican doctrine and thus endangers the status quo. Galileo is a wonderfully complex character in that, on one level, he displays near childlike joy in the search for knowledge which is utterly endearing, but such innocence is also located within a ferociously unpleasant ego for he is a man of ruthless and destructive conviction. His many faults are barely forgivable (he claims the modification of a new telescope as his own invention when clearly it isn't, he is an awful father, and often sees the new universe with only him at its centre), but Brecht/Ravenhill present a man who, in spite of such pragmatism, is somehow still one of us. To play any such figure, the actor must reduce the impressive 'whole' into much smaller and manageable thinking moments, and so whilst in this speech Galileo talks of popes and cardinals, a new age and a different universe, these are actually merely the results of many smaller thoughts stitched together – many hours of research, many hours of doubt. What drives his thirst for knowledge? Why is he content to be uncoupled from family, Church, State? What does Galileo now believe in?

Teacher of mathematics in Padua

Galileo   For two thousand years men have believed that the sun and all the stars in heaven spin around them.

The Pope, cardinals, princes, scholars, captains, merchants, women selling fish, school children: all believed they were sitting there motionless in the middle of that crystal ball.

We're heading off, Andrea, headlong into space. The old age has passed, this is a new age. For the past hundred years, it's as though humanity has been anticipating something.

Our cities are cramped, so are our minds. Superstition, plague. But now we say: that's the way it is, doesn't mean that's the way it has to stay. Everything's moving.

I like to think it began with the ships. Ever since man can remember all they did was creep along the coasts but then suddenly they left the coasts and sped out across the seas.

A rumour started: there are new continents. So we sent ships to the 'New World'. And now the continents laugh and say: the sea which we feared so much is a puddle.

A huge hunger has risen to explore the cause of everything: why a stone falls when we drop it and why it goes up when we chuck it up in the air. Every day we discover something new. Old people get young people to shout in their ears: what's the latest discovery.

We've found out so much but there's so much more to find. And so there's always new things for new generations to discover.

Where faith sat for thousands of years, there now stands doubt.

Playing with Grown-ups by Hannah Patterson

That's the problem isn't it?
Now we can have it all,
we're expected to bloody do it all

Playing with Grown-ups was first performed at Theatre503, London, on 14 May 2013 and was directed by Hannah Eidinow.

Context

Robert and Joanna and a nine-week-old daughter; what could be more perfect than that? Joanna thinks that there is quite a lot that could be better. Exhausted by endless sleepless nights and recovering from a Caesarean birth, she needs more than this to get her through. Robert invites their friend Jake (and Joanna's former lover) to dinner to cheer her up, and Jake brings his new vegetarian girlfriend, Stella. Stella is just sixteen. This extraordinary arrangement of ages, lives, despair and faded hope has echoes of Edward Albee's magnificent *Who's Afraid of Virginia Woolf*. However, the baby in this play is actually very real, but unloved and constantly wailing in the other room. Joanna wants out.

Acting notes

Robert's late thirties friend, Jake, reflects upon career, the passing of time and curse of approaching middle age. There is something unnerving about his perspectives, there is also something verging on the spectacularly inappropriate. For Joanna's new born baby is crying, Robert is barely able to keep awake due to a bad case of 'new Dad' tiredness, and in addition, Jake has brought along his new sixteen-year-old girlfriend – sixteen! Knowing that he is a 'dinosaur', or at least a soon to be dinosaur, what drives this man? Is his worldly cynicism a cover for something far more complex? Everything that was certain and fixed about his early career has now changed. Is the girlfriend part of the new 'rebrand' that he describes? His comment on how the university sector's move to the valuing of practice as opposed to previously valuing theory is very revealing in that it would seem that Jake is all talk, all theory, and that the move to practice has wrong-footed him.

For all of his party charm and cool-man-with-young-girlfriend glamour, it would seem that he is struggling to keep up. The challenge would be to smoothly deliver the 'I am coping' narrative alongside an inner feeling of growing anxiety.

Late-thirties

Jake   I'm not sure it's uppermost in their mind. At the moment. Your imminent book.

Beat.

Or film in general, for that matter. I mean how many students signed up for The Western this year, for God's sake? No, now it's all new digital cinema. New digital technology. New digital something. Film Studies won't last long.

Robert   (I can't believe that.)

Jake   We picked the wrong topics, Robert. We're dinosaurs already, and we aren't even middle-aged. Well I suppose we might be, it depends on when we die, but it's possible we're not yet middle-aged. And we're already dinosaurs.

Beat.

Gaming. Digital online gaming. Now that would have been a good choice. Or how to make films on a mobile. But nobody really cares about Fellini anymore.

Beat.

Some lecturers have been really very clever. Adding new on to everything. Feminism and new media. Horror and new digital cinema. Like Laura. Taking every course she can. Making her own films. They're crap, of course. No, I hate it, I really do, but she's thought ahead. And when it comes to choosing who stays and who goes, it's going to be about the future. Not the past.

Robert   (Like I said, it's just the conclusion really –)

Jake   Last meeting I had with the Vice-chancellor, it was all digital this, filmmaking that. Then you could easily charge nine thousand, he said, with a glint in his eye. More probably twelve, I said. Foolishly perhaps. With the right tutors.

Beat.

Yes, a rebrand, that's what I'm guessing. All practice. Very little theory. Looks like we could all be in trouble.

Red Velvet by Lolita Chakrabarti

It's like being at a crossroads –
a point of absolute, unequivocal change.
It makes my blood rush.

Red Velvet received its world premiere at the Tricycle Theatre, London, on 11 October 2102. It was directed Indhu Rubasingham.

Contexts

Lolita Chakrabarti's play is a true story about a young African-American actor called Ira Aldridge, who, when the great London stage actor Edmund Kean collapses on stage at the Theatre Royal, Covent Garden in 1833, is asked by the theatre's French manager to take over the playing of the coveted role of Othello. It is also a play about racism, for Aldridge's performance causes such an outcry that it leads to the theatre's ultimate closure.

Acting notes

In this speech, the theatre manager Pierre, is clearly very shaken by the realization that his promotion of Aldridge to the role of Othello has been a catastrophe. The Theatre Royal has closed and careers are now on the line. Aldridge and Pierre are on the verge of being hounded out of town like criminals. The obvious tension between the two men in this scene is immense. By closing the show, the once enlightened and fair-minded manager has given way to the overarching social pressures and norm of racism. Pierre betrays not only his friendship and association with the Ira, but also the man he once was. At every turn, Pierre's life is now changed forever. The challenge for the actor is to shape the emotional complexity of this moment. The pressure of external conflicting views is further amplified by his inner torment. The speech is delicately balanced between inner and outer rage.

French, white, thirty-five

Pierre   You push and you push but … you don't hear. Just yourself. Only ever yourself. I … you exploit yourself for all it's worth but when someone else dares to speak what they see, you refuse to acknowledge it. You think that work is your right. But everyone works hard, every damn one of us. Ambition drives us all and you have to prove your place like the rest of us. I've worked twice as hard because of what? – Gossip, accusations and now, I've earned my place. It's taken me years to get here. I won this role and then I invited you in. I took the gamble and all I asked was that you play it carefully, tone it down, toe the line for once. You never listen, how many times … ? This is not some huge political statement … you're not that important. This is about you. You have no one to blame but yourself, Ira. You've put me in an impossible position. The board, these are important men, they were outraged, indignant – the heat of your anger, your lack of respect … I am the first manager in the history of this theatre to go dark. I have done my very best. I even defended you, told them your influences have been different. Acting is about the freedom to play, I said, passion is felt and followed and our life experiences make each performer unique. I told them in the heat of the moment you lost yourself in the play, your true nature surfaced and you descended into …

Ira *lunges forward, outraged, out of control. He attacks* **Pierre**. *They are both furious and distraught.*

Pierre   Look at yourself. This is who you really are …

Acting notes

In this speech, the great actor Ira Aldridge confronts Pierre, a theatre manager, about art and accountability. The manager had previously been supportive of Aldridge's art, claiming to have been mesmerized and transfixed by it, but now, due to 'clear instruction', has been required to re-evaluate Ira's future. Ira senses that his career may now be, in effect, blocked by decisions based on his colour, as opposed to his skills as a performer. In a moment of heartfelt revelation, Ira explains that in the ten years it has taken him to find hard won success, his parents have waited for that moment – the moment that Ira has 'something to say'. Now, having contacted them with the joyous news of his success, and instructions to visit London, his career seems to be all but over. He describes an earlier attempt in his life, when as a fourteen-year-old child, the little timber theatre he played *Romeo and Juliet* was maliciously burnt down and destroyed. Ira feels that this memory has now come back to haunt him. The speech is striking for its simplicity; the actor must not be tempted to rage with despair, for such an emotion lacks clarity of thought. At this moment, Ira is very clear, almost rational, for he understands the situation. The technical balance required here is challenging; the actor must contain the character's obvious anger, show Ira's desperation, and set this alongside his sense of an ugly past that 'seems like yesterday'.

Ira   When I was a boy, there was this man, William Brown, he had
no one to follow either. Spent his life savings on a house, rundown,
basic but he had such passion he turned that house into a theatre. He
would serve cakes and punch in the back yard in the interval. His friend,
Jimmy Hewlett, was an actor – untrained, unpolished, worked as a tailor
uptown in the day but was burnin' up with talent. They dared too, Pierre.
You see Jimmy was cuttin' an' stitchin' in the day, Mr Brown did odd
jobs, I was at school but evenings we rehearsed and played *Romeo and
Juliet*, *Richard III*, *Henry V*. I was fourteen. We were rough but we had
passion … and we became real popular. Powers that be didn't like it
though and one night while we playin' in our tumbledown theatre and
our homemade costumes, they set fire to that house. It burned like paper.
The drier the wood, the quicker it burns. The noise was deafenin' –
screams, the flames catchin' further, shoutin'. Couldn't see my way out,
couldn't breathe and just when I thought I was done, Mr Brown grabbed
my hand, pulled me up from the floor and dragged me out into the
open air and look what he did. We just in the fire, Pierre … I've given
everything to get here. I have pushed and forced and played my way in.

The Resistible Rise of Arturo Ui by Bertolt Brecht, translated by George Tabori and revised by Alistair Beaton

Tonight no truth will be misrepresented.
No single moment censored or invented.
But blood brings blood, and blows will
answer blows.
So here's a gangster show to end all
shows...

This version of *The Resistible Rise of Arturo Ui* (based on Tabori's famous translation and revised by Alistair Beaton) was first performed at the Minerva Theatre, Chichester, on 29 June 2012 and transferred to the Duchess Theatre, London, on 18 September 2013. The production was directed by Jonathan Church.

Context

Brecht's much-loved allegorical satire charts Adolf Hitler's rise to power using 1930s Chicago as the sometimes hilarious, sometimes haunting, setting. Here we encounter the low-life political thuggery of the cauliflower trade, its market and people. The play is both outrageous and obvious; but the moment weedy Ui takes on board some unintentionally hammy performance coaching from an old has-been actor and leaves the stage in goose-stepping puffed-up glory, there is no doubt about its power to educate and entertain. Ui is an Everyman sucker lacking in intelligence, skill and charisma. His journey to power and the ease with which he attains it is hauntingly commented upon in the play's epilogue by the actor who plays him:

'So let's not drop our guard too quickly then: although the world stood up and stopped the bastard the bitch that bore him is in heat again.'

Acting notes

Brecht's play is so famous it hardly needs a guiding thought. Or so it would seem. But with reputation comes the danger of complacency. The actor can never presume to know how to play a particular role through piecing together bits of hearsay or second-hand renown. It is the given circumstances – the crucial facts – that are actually spectacularly revealing in this speech. A man almost on trial, giving witness, bearing testimony for his kind. This is a man of no importance who, as an exile, has worked hard to drag himself and his family out of the gutter. Brecht gives us Ui's mini-biography, or does he? There is, of course, the possibility that the words spoken are merely dressed-up emotive lies to strike a heartfelt chord within Mr Dogsborough. Is the rhetoric just too smooth? The circumstances just too heart-wrenchingly familiar? The actor must think clearly about what the character Ui really wants to achieve as a result of speaking this narrative. A deal with the police it would seem. So perhaps the speech is a bribe or threat, perhaps those unhappy years in the wasteland no more than a device. The choices for the actor are many. To presume one simple way through would be reductive and certainly diminish the dramatic possibility of this moment.

In the second speech given by the ghost of assassinated Ernesto Roma (with a bullet-hole in his forehead) we encounter something utterly terrifying – the truth spoken from the grave. Roma has been betrayed by his former sidekick and has paid the price. His speech clearly outlines how their friendship was destroyed by Ui and how at some point Ui will now see a 'bleeding world and full of hate' come after him. This long speech catalogues some of the many trials Roma has had to suffer and its emotional effect will only resonate if the list is imaginatively navigated by the actor. The terrible things described are offered with dignified grace, while the language used is devastatingly heartfelt. The actor will have to own the words but perhaps not reveal their horror. To do so will require a thinking, rather than overly demonstrative mechanism. It would be all too easy to play a two-dimensional rogue.

Ui   Sir, Mr Dogsborough –

Dogsborough   Get out.

Roma   Tut, tut. Let's not be hasty, now.
Let us be friendly, sir. It's Sunday, after all.

Dogsborough   I say, get out.

Young Dogsborough   My father says, get out.

Roma   Say away.
I've heard it said before.

Ui   Sir, Mr Dogsborough –

Dogsborough (*to his son*)
Go get the cops! And fetch the servants –

Roma   Don't leave us, sonnyboy.
Look out the window. You got company.

Dogsborough   So. Violence.

Roma   Oh no. No violence.
Just emphasis.

Silence.

Ui   Sir, Mr Dogsborough.
I am aware you don't know me from nothing,
Or maybe just by hearsay, which is worse.
You see before you, sir, a man misunderstood,
And almost done to death by sland'rous tongues,
His name besmirched by envy, and his dreams
Misrepresented by the meanness of a world
Replete with Jews and bicyclists. It was
A little over fourteen years ago
That me – that I – the simple son of Brooklyn
Came west without a job, a country boy Who cried 'Chicago,
I will lick you yet!' I wasn't altogether unsuccessful,
though I did it all alone but for the help
Of seven solid buddies standing by Without a pot to piss in like myself,
But firm in their determination, sir,
To carve themselves that little piece of goose Which God Almighty
cooks for every Christian. That tribe of seven's grown to thirty now,
And there'll be more of us, I guarantee.
You ask yourself, I guess: 'What's Ui want from me?'

Not much. One little thing, that's all I want.
I do not wish to be misunderstood no more
And treated like some greaseball racketeer,
Or buccaneer or
Whatever else they call me in this town.
I want respect.
(*Clears his throat.*) Not least from the police
Whom I have always so appreciated.
And that's the reason I am standing here,
And begging you – and I don't like to beg –
To say a word or two on my behalf
Whenever, God forbid, the heat is on.

Roma   Never ...
Your crimes will never blossom forth, Arturo.
Treason is bad manure. Go lie and slaughter.
Cheat all the Clarks and murder all the Dullfoots,
But don't touch your own men. Plot against
The world, but not against your fellow plotters, please.
Tell barefaced lies to everybody's face
But not the face you're facing in the mirror.
You struck yourself down when you struck me down!
I was devoted to you even in the days
When you were just a shadow falling on
A flophouse floor; and now I shiver in the draught
Of all eternity, while you go dining with
Your highfalutin friends. Treason has made you big:
Treason will make you fall. The way you did
Betray me, me, your friend and aide, you will Betray them all.
And in the end, Arturo, They'll betray you too.
Green grass grows over Ernie Roma.
Not over your disloyalty.
It's swinging in the breeze above the graves,
Like someone hung up by his toes.
It is Observed by all, this faithlessness of yours.
Especially by those who'll dig your grave.
The day will come when everyone you smashed
Will rise. Arise, arise will all the men
Already crushed by you and to be crushed tomorrow.
And they'll be marching down the street to you:
A bleeding world and full of hate.
And you will stand And look around for help.
I know. That's how I stood.
Then you will beg and bully, curse and lie.
No one will hear you. No one heard me cry.

Skin Tight by Gary Henderson

I wanted to see if I could live for just one
second without thinking about you. I wanted
to know that I could survive. That I could
forget you if I had to. I wanted to kill you
so they couldn't take you away from me.

Skin Tight had its world premiere at BATS Theatre, Wellington, New
Zealand, in 1994. It was produced by Epsilon Productions on 16 July
2013 at the Park Theatre, London, and directed by Jemma Gross.

Context

Elizabeth and Tom are poetic and passionate lovers who demonstrate
their romance through a sequence of very physical exchanges, sometimes
sensual, sometimes violent. What is certain is that they are irretrievably
in love. The play charts this in an extraordinary non-linear way, inspired
by New Zealand poet Denis Glover's poem *The Magpies*; we encounter a
curious dreamlike dance of lives past, at war and in love.

Acting notes

This is such an evocative speech, where images collide and the landscapes
of past memory and present reality mix indivisibly. It would be tempting
to soak up its rich evocative language and somehow give a grand narration
to these beautiful ideas – a sort of movie voice-over that honeys over each
idea with rich vowel sounds and a dreamy intent. But each memory, each
image, is the result of an experienced moment in life. Each one therefore
requiring what Stanislavski might describe as 'Given Circumstances' as
much as emotion memory, for every image is a pictorial molecule locked
away, storing all the information of that previous moment in every detail.
I suggest initial circumstantial auditing – the facts – the who, what, why,
where approach before engaging with an emotional response. It would be
far too easy to just drown in the emotion of this piece. The facts will be
the necessary architecture that will enable and hold the emotion. The last
line in the speech is significant. Why does Tom need or want to set 'ghosts
free'? This suggests something might actually be trapped.

Pakeha,* in the prime of his strength and vitality

Tom   It was a big part of me. Of both of us. While I was overseas it was like an anchor. The still point in all the chaos.

He gets to his feet. Moves around. She is lying on her stomach, listening to him.

Not just our farm, but this whole place. The plains. The Southern Alps. Names used to roll through my head like some kind of litany. Geraldine. Pleasant Point. Fairlie. Little nothing names full of magic. Up through Burke's Pass to the big lakes. Tekapo. Pukaki. And the rivers. The Waitaki. The Rangitata. And the big Rakaia churning milky and rich through the gorge. Names that seemed to invoke something vast. That recalled me to who I was and where I belonged. I knew when I came home it would be time to take the farm. Mum and Dad were ready to move into town. They were old.

He sits astride her back, strokes her hair and shoulders.

I remember that day on Orari Station. I was afraid to believe it too. I felt shattered. I hadn't slept. When you ran into my arms, I thought at any moment I would wake up, back in the desert, with the dream fading like sand through my fingers. For a few days we stepped carefully round each other, remember? Getting to know ourselves again. Gently feeling out the familiar things in each other.

He gets off and kneels beside her. She touches him as he speaks.

Then we moved on to the farm. There's something about the land. Something about belonging to it, sharing its history. Seeing the kids cutting across the far paddock to the willows for a swim after school, the same way we used to. Hearing the magpies in the pines of a morning, down the end of the house paddock.

Elizabeth   (Dive-bombing me when I went to hang the washing out.)

Tom   The river with its wide shingle bed, bringing down that rich alluvial mix from the Alps. It was fine land. You could crumble it in your fingers. Dig your toes into it. You could almost feel it humming with life. Good, wide, sunlit country. Somewhere a man could set his ghosts free.

---

*'Pakeha' describes a white New Zealander, usually born in New Zealand, of European descent.

Sucker Punch by Roy Williams

Jab. Double jab, cross. Jab, hook to body. One, two,
three, four, stepping forward jab and again. Hook, slip. And
again. Come on, double jab. Cross, hook, uppercut. Uppercut.

Sucker Punch received its first performance at the Royal Court Jerwood
Theatre Downstairs, London, on 11 June 2010. It was directed by Sacha
Wares.

Context

In his introduction to the play, Roy Williams states that he was 'watching
some programme on telly a few years back, which was a tribute to the
1980s' and that it was this programme that gave him the first initial idea
to write *Sucker Punch*. Williams suggests that 'they were discussing the
eighties like it was something that happened many years ago, but for me,
it was like yesterday. It seemed funny to me that my most recent past is
now a part of history.' The original Royal Court staging converted the
main house into a run-down boxing club, with a boxing ring and two
teenage hangers-on, West Indian boys called Leon and Troy. In the play,
the two boys' destinies take a fateful twist; like the heroic characters of
an ancient Greek tragedy, their once similar and ordinary lives change.
Troy goes to America to seek his fame and fortune as a newly designed
African-American star boxer, and Leon falls in love with his boxing
coach's daughter. In the course of the play, four years pass until the boys
meet again. Williams suggests 'It is not just boxers who need to keep their
guard up, it is all of us.'

Acting notes

The first speech by Leon from *Sucker Punch* is a graphic punch-by-punch
account of a boxing match. It is written very skilfully in that each sentence
seems to take on the rhythm of a gasped-for breath or dodged punch. As
the character gradually tires during the match, his speech patterning also
changes, with more repeated phrases and the use of the pronoun 'I'. In
may ways the speech has a triumphant feel to it, with words that seem to
suggest victory rather than defeat; but the actor should not just play the
heroic. To be in a boxing ring must be a terrifying experience and one that

is only endurable by a mix of both bravery and training. What is driving Leon's need to fight? Is it a need for sporting victory and medals for the mantlepiece or something far more personal?

In the second speech, the character Leon is clearly making phenomenal headway in his boxing career; prestigious matches are endlessly lined up by his enthusiastic coach, Charlie. Leon's reputation grows with every victory as he quite literally fights his way to the top. The actor must resist performing the all too easy fake boxing-swagger seen in bad movies, for while the times are going exceptionally well, there is also a terrible sense that at some point this bubble will burst. It would be important for the actor to measure Leon's understanding of his success against the wider sense of a career being merely used as a violent cash-generating machine. Does Leon really think that he is in some way immortal, or is he all too aware that success could be punched out of him in the next round?

Leon   The first fight I'm having is with some tall, skinny- looking kid. From the minute I step into the ring, he's staring me out, like I burgled his house. What am I doing here … ? Oh! He lands one right on me. I'm going dizzy, I'm all numb. I wanna go home. I'll keep out of his way.

Bell rings.

Crowd seem to like it when I move around. I'll go a bit faster then. They're lapping it up. Let's see if they like this. Bop my shoulders, spin my arm like Sugar Ray Leonard, now they're cheering, can't get enough. Skinny white boy don't know what to do with me! I get in a jab, and it hurts him, my first punch as well. A bit of fancy footwork now, I think. Crowd are loving it, I'm loving it. Another jab! Then a sweet uppercut! Skinny kid is down like a heap! I'm taking him out, me! My first ever fight, and I took him out. Fucking hell! Yes! What a feeling. Starting to like this. Next up is a fighter from Repton. Mark Saunders. Half-caste fighter from Brick Lane. Trying to find a way in here, but he's not having any of it. It's like he can see me coming. I go with the footwork. He can't keep up with me. I'm tiring him out, he's dazzled by my speed. That's it, that's it, keep him coming, keep him coming, now, have that!

He hits out with a flurry of punches.

Leon   Charlie set up a fight for me against Paul Kieron from Leeds.
Royal Albert Hall, thousands of seats, it was a seventy thirty split
seeing as Kieron was a former world-title holder. I take Kieron out in
five. Three months later, I'm there again, battering the hell out of Noah
Hunter in the fourth. And all we got was a forty split. The nerve! Earls
Court next, take on the UK champ, Shaun Callum, it was a fifty fifty
split, but it took me nine rounds to get that belt off him, and then six
in the rematch, which is where the real money is and I ain't lying, we
cleaned up! Spring of '87, Wembley Arena, fighting Paul Edwards, and,
yes, finally, this time we are the ones calling the shots, setting the pace,
walking away with the biggest purse. Seventy thirty in our favour and,
I swear, I can almost smell that dinero. I get the drop on Edwards in
the third, all too easy. Oh yes, without a doubt, I'm in my prime now.
Money is rolling in. My face on is on the front page of the *Boxing
News*. Giving Chas his first European title belt after I gave that Kraut
Werner a proper spanking. Oh yes! Now I have papers, magazines, telly
interviewing me nearly every week now. Asking me if I'm ever going
for the world title? Let me get this straight. Two title belts. Ten wins.
Six knockouts does the Pope live in Rome? Of course I am going for the
world title! I can't be touched, I won't be touched.

True Brits by Vinay Patel

The old lady on this train is looking at me,
Staring at me, she's been doing it since
new Eltham, I can feel her eyes on the
sweat of my neck. I turn to catch her out,
and she flicks her head back to her book,
like she's subtle, but she ain't .

True Brits received its world premiere at the Assembly Hall, Edinburgh on 31 July 2014, and was directed by Tanith Lindon.

Context

Sweeping between the paranoid London of 2005, and the euphoric city of the 2012 Olympics, Viany Patel's debut play explores both the love and violence of contemporary society, and asks what it actually means to be British in the post-9/11, post-7/7 generation. Eighteen-year-old Rahul loves the UK, is obsessed with Blur, and is in love. The only trouble is that after the London bombings of 7 July, he struggles to remain part of, and identify with, a British society that distrusts him on sight. Patel's dramatic style is also seemingly very low-key, almost conversational, but manages to present the dark yet funny struggles of a once carefree young man, now facing a changing world, one that conducts searches, or at least searches on young men like him, under the Prevention of Terrorism Act 2000.

Acting notes

Rahul's account of the ordinary, everyday encounter of daily racism and mistrust is as disturbing as it is unexceptional. 'The punch I can take, but the look … all these frightened half-glances'. It would be all too easy to turn this speech into a rant, or scream of despair, but what is extraordinary is that Rahul accepts his politicized identification from 'friendly guys' with machine guns as the unfortunate norm. The actor will have to protect the speech from becoming an all too transparent social comment, but rather, find a way of humanizing the context, removing it from the single doctrine of any manifesto or political party. This kid is just going about his daily business, but unfortunately the society that he lives in questions what that business is.

Eighteen, Estuary Accent

Mid-September 2005

Rahul   It's hot for September.

The old lady on this train is looking at me, staring at me, she's been doing it since New Eltham, I can feel her eyes on the sweat of my neck. I turn to catch her out, and she flicks her head back to her book, like she's subtle, but she ain't.

I wish she just punch me, y'know? The punch I can take, but the look … all these frightened half-glances they … they just …

I put on my most refined accent, and ask out loud:

'Excuse me, is this train to Charing Cross?'

Blank faces. In terms of desirability on public transport, I guess bombers are rivalled only by people that start conversations.

The old lady cocks her head as if to say, 'You're not fooling me!'

Fuck.

The station. I'm scanning about for Rhys, when I catch eyes with the fatter of two policemen standing lookout in the middle of the concourse. He nudges his partner, the Laurel to his Hardy, and make their way for me. I swing my bag around, my see-through bag, and there is nothing in it really, a jacket, a can of Coke for later and my wallet, but I know the drill by now.

'Excuse me, sir, we're conducting random searches under the Prevention of Terrorism Act 2000 …'

Inspection. One paws, the other scrawls.

Height? They guess five foot eleven, an inch more than last time. Clothing? Brown jumper, blue jeans, Adidas trainers. They're Reebok, but I'm not going to correct them. Intimate parts exposed? … No.

They are friendly guys these, Laurel's machine gun aside, doing a job that needs doing. The public are scared, they want to feel safe. I'm not saying that when a Brazilian electrician – on an expired visa by the way, I know it's not important, but just saying – when a Brazilian electrician gets shot through the head that we should just dismiss it. No. *But.* They're doing their best, they never asked for this.

'Where you come from?' says Hardy.

'Sorry?'

Laurel to the rescue: 'He means, "Where have you travelled from today?"'

They hand me the form so I can self-identity myself. The check boxes loom, all these options, and I can't help myself, I can't help but ask ...

'These are random searches?'

'Yes, sir.'

'How random are they?'

'Sorry?'

'I mean like, d'you have like a list? To keep track.'

'No.'

'Then how does anyone know that it's random?'

Wasted by Kate Tempest

I'm making a decision.
I'm changing things.
This is it.

Wasted received its world premiere at the Latitude Festival in July 2011, in a joint production between Paines Plough, Birmingham Repertory Theatre and The Roundhouse, and was subsequently revived in 2012 and 2013 as part of two Paines Plough national tours. It was directed by James Grieve.

Context

An extended sequence of stage and character descriptions occupy the first two pages of the published play. 'Sounds of London play out the speakers'. Ted is at a 'shitty little desk ... Charlotte in the staff room ... Danny is sitting on a dingy sofa ...'. Three ordinary lives that become, momentarily, a chorus who admit that they wish they had 'some kind of incredible truth to express', not heroes, but the kind of people who 'feel awkward in theatres'. Kate Tempest's debut play introduces three mid-twenties Londoners – a struggling teacher, a bored office worker and a musician in a rubbish band. Theatre of the ordinary; theatre of uneventful twenty-somethings, waiting-forever-waiting. Their lives blur into a sort of tragic hyper-ordinariness through the background noise of drugs, drink and pointless parties. It is only through their combined anonymous voice as 'chorus' that they try to work things out. Tempest's use of language and its near rap-like immediacy is both striking and effective. Will Ted, Charlotte and Danny ever find purpose or direction as easily as they find ecstasy at a good price?

Acting notes

Ted and Danny's speeches are the desolate hymns of a lost generation. There is such anger in both of them but in performance terms anger does not necessarily need to be all shout and strut, big gesture and rhetoric. These men are crippled by anger, frozen by it. Both men talk about what could have been, which implies that their imagination has at least visualized something better; both men are repulsed by their current useless context. What is it that has made them so inactive? What has made them not achieve what they have at least glimpsed in the subconscious?

Mid-twenties

Ted (*to* **Tony**, *about* **Danny**)   He ain't changed much, still believes he can have whatever he wants. Thinks he's gonna play guitar on seminal albums and tour America and write a cult fuckin' novel that'll change the way we think about our lives. Shit. He's one of my oldest friends, and I love him to pieces. I'd lie down and fuckin' die in the road for him – but sometimes, sometimes, he can be a bit of a knob. You know, I'm not being funny, but, you know, when he's with all his cool new 'creative' mates. They ain't real, Tony. They ain't like us. They sit around, with ironic trousers on and three haircuts each, waiting to be discovered.

What he don't realise is that in ten years, he'll be thirty five, one a them fuckers we used to laugh at at parties, gurning his face off, dribbling over some nineteen year old acid casualty called Sparkle telling himself he's still got it. He'll be there, giving it the old – I might be sensitive but I'm still dangerous – treating women like shit coz he hates himself for never having had the guts to put himself second and commit to one of 'em. It takes strength to commit, Tone, it really fuckin' does … Then, next thing he knows, he'll be forty-five, strung out from the cocaine and the booze and the MDMA, having panic attacks every night when he's on his own, coz he'll have realised that he's too old to be young anymore, and the world won't apply to him, and all the kids'll be listening to music he don't understand and suddenly all o' them interesting ideas he had, and all them exciting collaborations he was involved in, won't be half as fuckin' important anymore. He'll be worse off than me then. He'll have no seminal fuckin' work to wank off about, he'll be alone in his trendy flat, conducting imaginary interviews with imaginary journalists about imaginary masterpieces. And me? I'll be as miserable as I've always been, right there beside him.

Mid-twenties

Danny   You're lucky really.

If you'd have lived 'til now you would have just got fat and boring like the rest of us. You wouldn't have been no different.

You never got old enough to see your mate become the weirdo with a drugs lisp, looking like he's just found fishbones in his mouth, nodding to himself. In a Slammin Vinyl bomber jacket.

It used to feel like we was doing something that no one else had ever done. But really we was just getting fucked. And all them other kids that weren't cool enough to hang about with us, them ones we sold screwed up bits of clingfilm to for a tenner a go, they all grew up nicely, didn't they? They went off to uni and reinvented themselves and now they're doctors, replacing people's limbs in war zones, or they're professional cricketers, or they're working in the fuckin' city, blowing a ton on coke every night and fuckin' women that wouldn't even look at me if I was hanging in a gallery.

So you're lucky. Coz if you was still here, you'd have a habit, or depression, or anxiety attacks, or all three, and you'd be making secret plans to run away and start again in a new fuckin' country where no one knows how much of a fuckin' wreck you are, or, you'd be up to your neck in debt, fuckin' a bird that thinks you're a dick and checking your Twitter every twenty-two seconds to see if anyone's said anything about your fuckin' shit band. We used to be the fuckin' boys, mate.

The Whisky Taster by James Graham

*Well, let me put it this way. Today is our ... Uh, you
know, what would you – our 'assault' on marketing.*

The Whisky Taster was first performed at the Bush Theatre, London, on
26 January 2010. It was directed by James Grieve

Context

In his introduction to the play, playwright James Graham states that he
was wanting to write about being the age he was, in the city he was in,
feeling, as he did, that 'sometimes the whole thing was just too loud and
too colourful'. Barney and Nicola work in advertizing and are desperate
to secure an account for a new vodka brand. Barney has great marketing
savvy but he also has a neurological condition called synaesthesia, which
means that he experiences the world with hyper-real, often extreme sensa-
tions, especially in terms of colour. His proposed new blue, silver and
gold vodka campaign (informed by his condition), is a resounding success
and Barney gets the prestigious job. His task upon winning the contract is
to reinvigorate the fledgling culture of vodka and somehow make it more
like an established, traditional world-famous whisky.

Acting notes

In this speech, one of Barney's senior advertising colleagues gives him a
tough time after a sales pitch goes disastrously wrong. All the frustrations
and bitter resentments of a highly-charged working relationship come
spewing out. Though the speech is ostensibly about Malcolm's annoyance
in that moment of a failed sale, it actually requires emotional precision if
the true depth of Malcolm's anxieties are to be revealed. His annoyance
is not actually with Barney at all, but with the way his life has panned
out so far. Although he considers that he was born in a time that allowed
him to succeed, Malcolm clearly has doubts about his achievements, and
sees Barney as some sort of threat. The speech is therefore not about
Barney at all, but about Malcolm's own failure to survive in the hostile
and competitive world of marketing and advertising.

English, forties

Malcolm   No, I don't blame them, fuck it, if I were your lot, I'd fucking drink. Can't get a house, aw sorry, we've got them all, and shit, sorry, we've spent all that inherited wealth that's been passing down the generations on second homes and cars and holidays. But that's OK, you've been very patient, waiting your turn, but now – oh no! – there's no money left, we spent it, and there's less jobs, crikey, so tighten your belts. I would go away, travel, escape, but you can't really because we did that too much and now the planet needs saving. But the tragic thing is, the real crime, Barney, whatever you hate me for or blame me for, the biggest fucking crime of all is that none of you are angry enough to do anything about it. If this had happened to us, my God, we'd have set the place on fire. We were, we were changing everything, questioning everything, but you lot, God! You just shrug. And follow us. Do what we did. Go to uni still, even though when we went, it *meant* something. And you rent. From us. And pay your taxes, for our pensions and our retirement, none of which you will get to enjoy yourselves. That's why you drink. You're a stop-gap. An interval. And the worse thing is you don't even care. But *you,* Barney, I see it, you do care. And you / hate me for it.

Geoffrey Colman is Head of Acting at the Royal Central School of Speech and Drama. As an acting coach, he has collaborated with many national and international theatre, film and TV practitioners, and has a longstanding association with the Theatre Royal Haymarket as a 'resident master'. Recent award-winning theatre credits include *I Loved You and I Loved You* (Sweetshop Revolution / National Theatre Wales), *Justitia* (Jasmin Vardimon Company / Peacock Theatre, London), *PARK* (Jasmin Vardimon Company / Sadlers Wells, London). TV/film coaching credits include *Britain's Next Top Model* (Sky Living), *Mother of Invention* (HBO/Sky 1), extensive work with BAFTA award-winning mentalist & hypnotist, Derren Brown, including *Miracles For Sale* (Channel 4), *Fear & Faith/Placebo* (Channel 4), *Apocalypse* (Channel 4), *The Push*, (Channel 4 / Vaudeville Productions), and also with mentalist and illusionist Katherine Mills *Mind Games* (Watch TV). Film coaching includes *Kick Ass 2* (Marv Films/Universal Pictures, directed by Jeff Wadlow). Geoffrey Colman writes for The Stage and lectures on a wide range of performance-related issues (National Portrait Gallery, National Theatre, ICA, etc.). He also regularly broadcasts on BBC (Radio 3/Free Thinking, Radio 4/The Why Factor, and BBC World Service/Weekend etc.). Bloomsbury Methuen Drama recently published his introduction to Steven Berkoff's *One Act Plays*.